THE EVOLUTION OF A MOST PECULIAR SONGWRITER

A Guide to Songwriting and a Memoir

ARNOLD D. CRIBARI

The Evolution of a Most Peculiar Songwriter
Copyright © 2024 Arnold D. Cribari
Published by Free Agent Press
All rights reserved.

No portion of this book may be reproduced in any form without written permission from the publisher or author, except as permitted by U.S. copyright law.

This publication is designed to provide accurate and authoritative information in regard to the subject matter covered. It is sold with the understanding that neither the author nor the publisher is engaged in rendering legal, investment, accounting or other professional services. While the publisher and author have used their best efforts in preparing this book, they make no representations or warranties with respect to the accuracy or completeness of the contents of this book and specifically disclaim any implied warranties of merchantability or fitness for a particular purpose. No warranty may be created or extended by sales representatives or written sales materials. The advice and strategies contained herein may not be suitable for your situation. You should consult with a professional when appropriate. Neither the publisher nor the author shall be liable for any loss of profit or any other commercial damages, including but not limited to special, incidental, consequential, personal, or other damages.

Edited by Shawn Cribari
Book Design by FreeAgentPress.com

ISBN: 978-1-946730-32-9 (hardcover)
ISBN: 978-1-946730-33-6 (paperback)
ISBN: 978-1-946730-34-3 (e-book)

Published by Free Agent Press
FreeAgentPress.com
Satsuma, Alabama 36572
VID: 20250402

". . . the writing of a song is a sublime achievement, a triumph of the spirit."

Paul Zollo

Cover Photo: The author and his daughter, Maria Cribari, when she was 9 years old. Maria, as an adult, sings on the recordings of many of the author's songs.

CONTENTS

1. You Can Do It 1
2. In the Beginning: Love and Death 5
3. Does Anyone You Know Personally Write Songs? 11
4. Songwriting Advice from Cousin Donna 15
5. Shawn 19
6. My Methodology and Tips for Writing Songs 23
7. My Twilight Time: A Time for Creativity 33
8. Irving Berlin's Nine Rules for Writing Popular Songs 37
9. Songwriters on Songwriting 39
10. The Thrill of Victory and The Agony of Defeat 43
11. Jumpin' Up and Down Excited 47
12. Rings of Saturn/Cinderella's Eyes 57
13. Different Genres of Music and Miscellaneous Songs 67
14. Jean-Christophe 77
15. Cultivate Your Garden 81
16. Final Thoughts 83
List of Songs with QR Codes 89
List of Music Videos on YouTube 97
Bibliography 99
About the Author 101
Epilogue: Ode to the New Jersey HiRailers 103

CHAPTER 1

YOU CAN DO IT

THE FACT THAT YOU have picked up this book and have started reading it indicates that you might have some interest in songwriting.

You can do it. If I can do it, you can do it.

I do not read music. Strictly speaking, I am musically illiterate. And yet, I have written over 50 songs that I treasure and most of my family and friends like a lot. Most of my acquaintances that have heard my original songs at Open Mics and model train shows, or on YouTube and other online music platforms like Spotify, iTunes, Apple Music, TikTok, Pandora, Amazon Prime, and Instagram/Facebook also like them a lot.

I am a model train nut as well as a songwriting and Open Mic nut. One of my best songs, "Who Am I (Rollin' By)," is about model railroading. I have performed that song for thousands of people at train shows and even more have heard it worldwide, on the above-mentioned music platforms, and as part of my music video, on the O-Gauge Railroad Magazine On-Line Forum and on YouTube. If you want to watch that music video, it's available on YouTube under my name, Arnold D. Cribari. If you do so, please contact me by emailing me at ADCSong1951@gmail.com and give me your honest feedback, good or bad.

I hope and pray I've piqued your interest about songwriting enough that you will read more of this book—I love spreading the gospel about songwriting.

If you are just starting to write songs, please keep the following in mind.

You may find out, like I did, that the initial reaction you get from some people when you tell them of your songwriting, is different from the response to other activities. What I'm about to say is particularly true if they believe you have little, if any, involvement with music.

Several people, who had always been very respectful towards me, rudely rolled their eyes when I told them I was writing songs. I've had a lot of interests throughout my life, and no one rolled their eyes when I told them I was playing golf or tennis, taking up archery (shooting targets, not animals, with a recurve bow), building a model railroad, joining a hiking group, or playing guitar and singing.

I took their rolling of the eyes as saying "Oh no, not one of those," "You just think you are a songwriter," "You can't possibly be any good at it," or "You must suck at songwriting." These people rolled their eyes before listening to any of my songs, which I thought was very strange.

Another bizarre reaction was from a relative who will remain nameless. He is generally very witty and charming, an extrovert, has a great sense of humor, and is very well liked. He was going on and on about how much he loved the musical *Hamilton* for over 45 minutes and insisted on playing several of its songs. When he finished, I mentioned that I had recently written a new song and asked if he would like to hear it. It was so bizarre the way he emphatically refused to hear it. Even his wife was shocked at his bizarre negative response. I replied that I was fine with his refusal to hear my new song and reassured him that I would never share any of my songs with him for the rest of my life.

His response was so that I wonder if he was a conduit for some mysterious force that didn't want him to hear my new song. Another possibility is that he was envious of me having done something so creative as writing a song, or might have simply thought that the song had to suck because I wrote it. I will never ask him, so I will never know why he reacted the way he did.

CHAPTER 2

IN THE BEGINNING: LOVE AND DEATH

LOVE AND DEATH GOT me started with writing songs. It started for me in 1985 when I wrote and delivered a eulogy for my father, Arnold D. Cribari (my birth name is Arnold D. Cribari, Jr.).

That was the first time I ever did any creative writing outside of a school assignment, and that didn't happen very often.

I can't remember a single example of any school-related creative writing assignment. If I ever did one, it wasn't very meaningful to me. However, writing my father's eulogy was deeply meaningful to me.

I began writing the eulogy with pencil and paper. It flowed from me without any hesitation, as if some mysterious force was putting the words in my brain.

My father was the sole breadwinner in my family, except for the modest income my mother got from giving piano lessons and being a beneficiary of a small trust fund. My parents, mostly my father, paid every penny of my education at Columbia College in New York City and Albany Law School in Albany, NY.

The Evolution of a Most Peculiar Songwriter

My father was a good man and had great charisma. He was handsome, athletic, and very good in sports like baseball, tennis, and golf (I'm pretty good at those sports, too). I consider my father, in appearance and persona, to be a cross between Dean Martin and Joe DiMaggio. All three were Italian—the tall, dark, and handsome type—but, in truth, my father could not sing as well as Dean Martin, and he certainly could not hit as well as Joe DiMaggio.

Below are photos of my parents, Arnold D. Cribari and Idaehla Cribari, taken around 1930 when they were approximately 21 years old.

Here is a photo of my parents at my graduation from Columbia College in 1973.

In the Beginning: Love and Death

My father's goodness was also evident from the fact that he stayed married to my mother, who had a few severe bouts of bipolar disorder during her adult life.

Knowing my father's core goodness and his commitment to his family, upon learning of his death, my eulogy for him flowed through me. In that eulogy, I was my father's lawyer and made the case, on his behalf, before God, that my father deserved a place in Heaven. I wrote it in a flood of tears and delivered it at the St. Peter and Paul Catholic Church in the Fleetwood section of Mt. Vernon, New York.

Writing that eulogy was the very beginning of my evolution as a songwriter.

Sometimes, when I feel I have written something special, I think that something or someone else wrote it, or at least helped me write it.

For instance, regarding the eulogy, my father had an extraordinarily talented and successful older brother, Wolfe Cribari. They were very close. Wolfe was a great trial lawyer, actor, and singer—a true Renaissance Man—who was highly regarded by judges, lawyers and others in his community from the late 1920s until his death in 1966. His oldest daughter, Camille Cribari Linen, wrote a lovely book in 2022 about her father entitled *Wolfe with an E (An Episodic Journey Through an Exceptional Life)*.

After reading Camille's book, I wonder if the spirit of the deceased Wolfe Cribari wrote that eulogy for my father, using me as a conduit.

I have had similar thoughts about the creation of some of my original songs. Did I write them or was it someone from among the beloved dead, or some other mysterious force, that wrote them?

SUNRISE AT THE SHORE/GLORY BORN

My mother, Idaehla Short Cribari, died in May 1991. In August 1991, my wife, two young children, and I went on our perennial summer vacation at Long Beach Island, New Jersey. Early one morning during that vacation, I took my guitar with me to the beach and watched the sunrise. Music and lyrics came to me.

I remember returning to the beach cottage and asking my wife what the pink/purple color that I saw in the sunrise was called. She replied that it was mauve. Then I wrote, "Clouds of pink and mauve adorn," which is the first line of lyrics for my song, "Sunrise at the Shore" written in 1991:

Clouds of pink and mauve adorn,
The brightening sunrise at the shore,
Another day is glory born.

Light of pink and mauve adorns,
Waves of passion on the shore,
My love for you is glory born.

See the empty shells, washed upon the shore,
Gone are those we loved so well.
Lost are those we held before.

Let me see them once again.
Let me touch them once again,
Hold me, never let me go again,

Love me, we may never love again,
Let me love you once again,
Like the sunrise at the shore,
I will love you every morn.

Waves of pink and mauve adorn,
Empty shells along the shore,
Another day is glory born,
My love for you is glory born.

Around 2013, I changed the title of this song to "Glory Born."

All of my songs mentioned in this book are available on all streaming platforms under my name, Arnold D. Cribari. For your convenience, you can also access them by turning to the List of Songs with QR Codes at the back of the book.

For instance, you can hear "Glory Born" beautifully sung by my daughter, Maria Cribari, by scanning the QR Code for it and uploading the song on your smartphone.

My first cousin, Donna Cribari, has composed full-length musicals, taught music at Marymount Manhattan College, and served as the musical director of many musical theater productions in the Westchester County, New York area. When I shared the lyric sheet and recording of "Glory Born" with Donna, she asked me with an accusatory tone (that I now take as a compliment): where did the line "My love for you is glory born," come from? My answer was, I don't know.

After drafting about the first ten pages of this book, an expression dawned on me that I thought could be a good title for a new song—"Jumpin' Up and Down Excited." I made a note of that title.

I then began writing that song.

The reason I'm mentioning this new song now is to show how ideas for songs can suddenly pop into the songwriter's head, surprisingly and unexpectedly.

"Jumpin' Up and Down Excited" is the subject of Chapter 11.

CHAPTER 3

DOES ANYONE YOU PERSONALLY KNOW WRITE SONGS?

IF THERE IS SOMEONE in your family or that you personally know that writes songs, that can be the impetus for you to write your first song. It could be a friend, a fellow Open Mic performer, an acquaintance, or a relative.

My cousin, Donna Cribari, contributed to my motivation to start writing songs in 1991.

Donna is about 10 years older than me. When she was a young woman, I remember attending a public performance of hers during which she played guitar and sang her song "How Would You Know?" I liked that song a lot and still do.

To my knowledge, no one else in my family wrote songs even though other relatives of mine performed them, including my mother, who taught piano to my two older sisters and me and other kids in our neighborhood. I hated playing piano back then because I much preferred playing baseball and other ball-related games, and I did not like the songs my mother had me play on the piano like "Beautiful Dreamer" by Stephen Foster. After two miserable years of playing and practicing songs like that for my mother, she finally let me quit playing piano.

I might have felt differently about playing and practicing piano if my mother had me play songs I liked. For instance, when my now 37-year-old daughter, Maria, took piano lessons as a child, her piano instructor had her play the theme song from the *Addams Family* TV show. I would have loved playing a cool song like that when I was a child.

If I knew back then that 35 years later, I would start writing songs, off and on, for the rest of my life, I would have continued playing piano. This would have enabled me to read and write musical notation and benefited me as a songwriter. Although I don't read music, I do play chords on the guitar, which has helped me write songs.

My late beautiful older sister, Idaehla, not only mastered the piano, but she was also an excellent singer and a fine finger picking guitarist who played and sang many folk songs in the style of Joan Baez. Idaehla even recorded herself using a reel-to-reel tape recorder. My wife, Shawn, recently told me that Idaehla said that she played and sang folk songs at Greenwich Village coffee houses while she was a student at NYU. However, to my knowledge, Idaehla never even attempted to write a song. This surprises me because she was very familiar with the folk music of the early and mid-1960's and was a good writer as an NYU student with a double major in Art History and English Literature.

Still, it's a bit of a mystery to me that Idaehla never wrote a song. Maybe it's because she excelled at performing and was content doing that.

The awareness of one's mediocrity as a singer or musician can motivate one to write songs, like it did for me.

In the same way that my cousin, Donna, was the songwriter pioneer in my family, her sister, Camille Cribari Linen, and Camille's husband, Lou Del Bianco, were the book writing pioneers in my family. As mentioned earlier, Camille has recently written a book, *Wolfe with an E,* about her father (my uncle), Wolfe Cribari. Before that, Lou Del Bianco wrote a book, *Out of Rushmore's Shadow (The Life of Luigi Del Bianco)*, about his grandfather, Luigi Del Bianco, who was the principal carver of Mount Rushmore. Lou was interviewed on the *CBS Sunday Morning Show* about his book.

CHAPTER 4

SONGWRITING ADVICE FROM COUSIN DONNA

MY FIRST COUSIN, **DONNA CRIBARI**, gave me direct and honest feedback about my songs. That really worked for me because I knew she had my best interests at heart, and she had an enormous positive impact on my life that transcends songwriting (more about this in Chapter 5). When I shared my first few songs with Donna, she was kind and compassionate and told me they were nice songs of a personal nature—and that it was best to keep them private.

Soon thereafter, when Donna sensed that I was taking songwriting more seriously and wanted to write a song that has the potential to be a hit and share my songs with others in public venues, she told me the following:

- It is usually best if songs use plain language and are focused and short (not more than 4 minutes).
- One should pick universal themes that many can relate to.
- It is usually best to keep "God" out of it.
- If you want to write hits, you need a hook—a catchy melody, rhythm and/or lyrics.

I took Donna's advice to heart and did my best to write such a song. When I reconvened with Donna, she was tough. When I wrote a song that had too much in it and lacked focus, she said if I want to do that, don't write songs, write poetry. When I had too many images in the bridge of one of my early songs, "Down by the Reservoir" (the original title was "The Croton Reservoir"), including an image that God was "peeking at me through the crescent moon" while I was fishing in a rowboat at the reservoir, Donna (who is a former nun) told me, "Take God out of it." You can hear the revised final version of "Down by the Reservoir" sung by me, by scanning the QR Code for it at the back of the book.

When I wrote a spiritual song entitled "Prayer for the Homeless" that had the powerful, but rather harsh, lyric "His crown of thorns, the awful stench, and all the filth he lives in," Donna told me, "Leave him (the homeless man), alone!"

I immediately picked up pencil and paper and changed that lyric and re-wrote other lyrics in "Prayer for the Homeless."

During my first two years of songwriting, Donna also told me I was spending too much time on the words, and I should spend more time on the music because listeners pay more attention to the music than the words. She also said that my songs sounded alike. Then, she told me to write a waltz. Initially, I thought, why would Donna tell me to write an old-fashioned song like a waltz? Donna explained that a waltz is a song with a 3/4-time signature, which made it different from the music I was composing up to that point in time.

For the next two weeks I spent most of my spare time humming tunes in 3/4 time into my attorney's dictating unit. Then, while vacationing with my family at Disney World, I wrote the music and lyrics for my first waltz: "Earthrise."

I remember my arranger, Kinny Landrum, telling me twenty years later that he could turn my music and lyrics for "Earthrise" into a simple ballad, or he could make it "as big as a house." I opted for him to make it as big as a house, meaning a full orchestra for dramatic accompaniment.

You can access my music video, "Earthrise," sung by Maria Cribari, on YouTube under my name.

I had a practical attitude about this early songwriting advice I got from Donna. She was the only songwriter I personally knew back then, and she was clearly very good at it. I compared it to my past experiences with baseball and golf. If I wanted to be a better baseball player, I got advice from my baseball coach and my father. Same with golf—if I wanted to be a better golfer, I would get advice from my father and, later on, I would pay to have a golf lesson from a golf pro at a driving range.

Donna was my songwriting coach during the first couple of years I wrote songs from 1991 to 1993.

I'm torn, however, about whether Donna's teaching style with me is the best way to guide an aspiring songwriter. It may depend on the songwriter's upbringing and background, but her tough truthfulness sure worked for me. One reason for that is the fact my mother instilled in me as a young child the idea that constructive criticism is a good thing. Also, I knew Donna was brilliant and had enhanced my life in myriad ways. I'm so glad that I wrote "Lovely Donna"—one of my first songs—which describes how Donna enchanted me when she would get on her hands and knees and play with me at our grandmother's house when I was a little boy.

When I was in my mid-twenties, I had lunch with Donna at McDonalds and told her I was sad because a relationship I had with a woman broke off. (I had numerous unrequited love experiences, which is great fodder for a songwriter). A few days after that lunch, Donna asked me if I would like to join her to see a play in New York City and would I mind if four single girls joined us. That was music to my ears.

CHAPTER 5

SHAWN

I'M NOT STUPID. I'M also a hopeless sentimental romantic and was familiar with Paul Simon's early hit, "Red Rubber Ball," with its healing lyric: "Now I know you're not the only starfish in the sea."

I joined Donna to see that play with her four single women friends, and met a beautiful young brunette who, as soon as she laid eyes on me, never stopped smiling at me.

Of course, I sat next to this beautiful brunette with the stunning smile during the play. I was oblivious to what was going on during the play (I was shocked to later find out that it was about African female circumcision).

The brunette, formerly Shawn Kennedy from Troy, NY, who was then living with a girlfriend in an apartment in White Plains, NY, was charming. Very early on, it was readily apparent that she was smart, well-educated, cultured, and had good values, as well as being a physically beautiful, slender brunette.

She has exquisite taste, not only in men (LOL), but also in the arts and music. I have received invaluable feedback from her regarding all my original songs and now I know how best to conduct myself during the feedback process—by respectfully making appointments with her to get it, and never before her morning coffee (which could turn out to be life-threatening for me).

Advice from my wife, Shawn, who was born and bred on Rodgers & Hammerstein, includes the following:

   i. Don't be preachy.
   ii. Be willing to take out "your darlings" (your favorite lyrics that might detract from the song's focus or that otherwise don't quite work).
   iii. Metaphors are great, provided they completely work. If not, either delete the metaphor or come up with one that totally works in the song.
   iv. Often, less is more.

Shawn supports me and my songwriting by not only continuing to give me her invaluable feedback and advice (about this book as well as my songs), but also by singing my original songs and our favorite cover songs at local, and not so local, Open Mics and gigs.

CHAPTER 6

MY METHODOLOGY AND TIPS FOR WRITING SONGS

1. When you write songs, they can be fiction, nonfiction, or a combination of both in one song.

2. It is helpful to pick a subject that you know a lot about when you write the song. Picking a subject that you know about for the song might help you come up with a catchy tune and lyrics that express the emotion you feel about the subject relatively quickly. I experienced this writing my song, "Who Am I (Rollin' By)" about model trains. I started out with the goal of writing a Johnny Cash–like song about real trains and was getting nowhere. I said to myself, I know very little about real trains, but a lot about model trains—then I wrote that model train song in a few hours.

3. What if you don't know much about the subject and still want to write the song? You can Google it. For example, in "Whiskey and a Woman So Fine," the first verse mentions the cattle drive known as the Chisholm Trail. I did not know anything about the Chisholm Trail until I Googled cattle drives and then went on Wikipedia to learn about the Chisolm Trail. "Whiskey and a Woman So Fine" is a story-song involving reincarnation. Its structure is similar to "Highwayman," one of my favorite songs written by Jimmy Webb.

4. A willingness to be transparent about one's feelings may be a prerequisite for writing songs. One of my friends, who is a very smart singer, guitarist, and author, rarely attempts to write a song because he fears making himself vulnerable by expressing his feelings in a song. Until my friend recently mentioned this to me, it never occurred to me that a willingness to bare one's soul may be important to get started as a songwriter.

5. Most listeners get hooked more on the music (the melody, the tune, and/or the rhythm) than the lyrics, so it is a good idea to make the music a priority.

6. To come up with good lyrical ideas, use Sheila Davis' technique known as "clustering" which is described in her book, which I regard as my songwriting Bible, *Successful Lyric Writing (A Step-by-Step Course & Workbook)*. Examples of clustering appear in Chapters 11 and 12 of this book.

7. When you initially cluster lyrical ideas, don't edit them. While editing is ultimately very important, to edit during the early clustering stage might thwart creativity. Instead, write down every lyrical idea that comes to mind. Even if your initial lyrical ideas consist of clichés or drivel, they may lead you, through an association process, to much better lyrics that you will also write down. This is especially likely to happen after the subconscious mind kicks in.

8. Start thinking about the structure of the song that makes sense when keeping the tune and the lyrical ideas in mind. The various ways a song can be structured is another subject covered in depth in the Sheila Davis book, *Successful Lyric Writing*.

9. Modulation (changing key) or going from major to minor, or minor to major, maybe in the middle, or in the bridge, of the song, are simple ways to add drama and musical variety to your songs and hold the listener's interest.

10. All you need is a tune and a few good lyrical ideas to begin the song. Over the next few days, you may find that more lyrical ideas will come to you from the subconscious mind—when you are driving, taking a bath, going for a walk, or otherwise living your life—and not even trying to write or finish the song.

11. I am unable to write the notes (musical notation) for my songs. In the past, I used a portable cassette player and now use the Voice App on my smartphone to record my ideas for tunes and lyrics so I don't forget them.

12. Sheila Davis says in *Successful Lyric Writing* and *The Songwriter's Idea Book* that a smart way to start a song is to come up with a fresh, memorable title, and to make sure that what the title says is what your song is *really* about. A song title can be the most important lyrical line or phrase in the chorus of the song where the musical hook is most prominent. You can live your life and then simply hear, see, or dream up a potentially great title for a song and make a note of it.

13. James Taylor was interviewed a few years ago during a Red Sox/Yankees baseball game. The sportscaster asked him some questions about writing songs in connection with his new song at that time entitled "Angels of Fenway." When asked what comes first, the tune or the lyrics, he replied that most of the time the tune comes first and is often very easy and quick to compose. However, it may take years for him to complete the lyrics of a song. Instead of intentionally deciding on a specific subject for a song, he keeps himself open regarding his thoughts and experiences, and after he gets some ideas and is inspired, he writes a song.

14. I am enamored with Paul Simon, listening to his YouTube interviews and marveling at the beauty of his lyrics and melodies. I have used his songbook, *The Songs of Paul Simon*, so much that the binding has disintegrated and the book is held together by a large binder clip. Paul has mastered songwriting in American Folk Rock. I often perform covers of his songs at Open Mics and now gigs. Although I am not very familiar with his other types of songs like "Graceland,"

his original African music, or his Caribbean music, I know that these other examples of work by Paul have received high critical acclaim.

15. During one of his YouTube interviews, Paul Simon mentioned that he likes to have at least three varieties of music in each of his songs to hold the listener's interest. This can be done by having one type of music for the verses, another type of music for the chorus, and a third type of music for the bridge of the song. A good example of this is Paul Simon's masterpiece, "Bridge Over Troubled Water."

16. Another thing about Paul Simon's songs is the richness of the poetry in his lyrics. I recently heard him say in a YouTube interview that during college, he majored in English Literature, not music. I believe that a good background for an aspiring songwriter might be English Literature or some other literature. However, the good news is that a college major is not a requirement for writing good lyrics. Paul McCartney never went to college and John Lennon went to Liverpool College of Art but didn't graduate—and the Beatles' lyrics are just fine (a gross understatement). *Successful Lyric Writing* by Sheila Davis provides a lot of good information regarding poetic devices and figurative language (metaphors, similes, different forms of rhyme, etc.) to help an aspiring songwriter write better lyrics.

17. Music can truly be humanity's universal language. What better way to bring the world together? This gets me very excited and motivated me to write this book.

18. Be open. This is something which seems to come naturally to me and is essential in order for my brilliant music mentor, Kinny Landrum, to be able to work with me as my arranger, synthesizer, studio keyboard player—and to record and produce my songs.

19. Understand "melisma" and "scansion." Melisma happens when there is more than one note of music per syllable. It's usually best to minimize melisma by having only one note per syllable; and to use more than one note per syllable sparingly and only for dramatic effect—such as at the end of a line of lyrics to emphasize a particular word. Scansion involves the accents on the syllables of the words. The goal is to have the lyrics sung naturally with the accents on the proper syllables. I learned about melisma and scansion from taking a songwriting class that Kinny Landrum taught, as well as from my many private coaching sessions with him about my songs.

20. One of my best tips for writing better songs is simply to ask your listeners to give you their honest feedback—good or bad—about your song. If you get bad feedback, please thank them for it.

    Why would a songwriter want bad feedback about his/her songs? If you get consistent negative feedback regarding anything about your song, then you have a great opportunity—provided you are willing to do more work—to improve it.

    Share your original songs at Open Mics and ask some people in the audience to listen carefully to your songs as you perform them. If you get numerous people saying that something in your song does not work, then consider re-writing or modifying your song. Openness and humility are helpful for writing good songs. Don't let your ego get in the way of improving your song. Put your ego aside, and welcome feedback from anyone willing to listen. Then, decide what changes, if any, you want to make.

I found that women in the audience at Open Mics tend to be better listeners than men in providing me with this invaluable honest feedback. My dear wife, Shawn, is my #1 for giving me this honest feedback, but other women on occasion have provided this feedback for me. Jody Cole, a friend of mine who is an outstanding singer and guitar player, did this for my song, "Oh Good Earth." I asked her to listen carefully before I sang it at an Open Mic several years ago. She did, and then told me afterwards that she liked the song but suggested that I add more musical variety within the song to hold the listener's interest. I modified the song, changing key in the middle of the song from major to minor, and back to major. This relatively small modification substantially improved the song. I greatly appreciate Jody's honest feedback that led to this improvement. You can access my music video, "Oh Good Earth," sung by Maria Cribari, on YouTube under my name.

21. Little changes to a song can make a big difference. Stephen Sondheim said in his books, *Finishing the Hat*, and *Look, I Made a Hat*, that even a single preposition or syllable in a song can be monumental.

22. Songwriting is an all-absorbing activity for me. I can get very emotional while writing a song—even being moved to tears when writing a humorous song. It's also intense for me because it can make me feel, when in the throes of it, that I'm doing something wonderful.

23. I suppose that my highly passionate experience in writing songs may be more than a bit odd, hence the title of this book *The Evolution of a Most Peculiar Songwriter* which is an homage to Paul Simon's song, "A Most Peculiar Man." I hope, however, that my life will not end in the same sad way as the life of Paul's most peculiar man in his song.

24. Don't be surprised if, when you first discover that you can write songs that are emotionally moving for you, you start doing it like a mad scientist. This happened to me in 1991 when I wrote a song a day for a while. I'm a pack rat and saved my numerous drafts of the lyric and chord sheets for these songs and my primitive recordings of them. Most of them were medieval in their music style making me think, to this day, that I may be a reincarnated medieval troubadour. Indeed, one of my first songs has the title "Poor Troubadour." My only experience with anything medieval was taking the class, Medieval History, at Barnard College as a Columbia College senior. I liked it, and got a decent grade, but otherwise, it was uneventful. My sister, Idaehla, had a record of Gregorian chants which I heard and kind of liked. Simon and Garfunkel had a song on their "Wednesday Morning, 3 AM" album entitled "Benedictus" that sounded like a Gregorian chant. It was very nice, but not an earth-shattering experience for me to hear.

25. Well, thank God that my "a song a day" songwriting is no longer! If I continued to do that for more than a couple of weeks, it would have surely destroyed my marriage. Speaking of marriage, my advice (as a former divorce litigator and now a collaborative divorce lawyer and mediator) is please don't drive your spouse crazy with your compulsive need for feedback from him/her regarding your songs. In other words, don't hound your spouse, or anyone else for that matter, to get feedback.

26. Now, I only write songs when inspired to do so, which might happen a few times per year, at most. This works well for me at this time in my life. When it happens, I feel like I'm truly living life to its fullest, and that is what I wish for you.

CHAPTER 7

MY TWILIGHT TIME: A TIME FOR CREATIVITY

I HAVE LEARNED TO EMBRACE my mild case of insomnia. It's mild because I almost always fall asleep for a few hours,, wake up briefly, then usually get back to sleep…but not always. When I don't fall back to sleep, instead of cursing to myself that I'm not getting enough sleep, I accept it—even if I'm not happy about it. I am mindful of the potential for deriving benefits from it—specifically, that I often get my best ideas during this twilight time. An example of this occurred while I was writing this chapter.

I know that many people experience insomnia. Don't despair if this happens to you. Consider accepting it and be open to the possibility that it may become one of your most creative times.

My twilight time has been one of my best times for coming up with titles and subject matter for songs. It's also been great for "finishing the hat," a metaphor used by the great songwriter, Stephen Sondheim, for finishing a song. (*Finishing the Hat* is the title of a book by Stephen Sondheim, as well as the title of his largely autobiographical song in his musical, "Sunday in the Park with George.")

Irving Berlin, who was a prolific songwriter, suffered from insomnia. He lived to the age of 101. This tells me that not only is insomnia a potential time for creativity, it is also not necessarily a danger to one's health. I'll take 101 years of life provided I can be relatively physically and mentally active and robust for most of those 101 years.

Stephen Sondheim discovered that going in and out of sleep were times that were ripe for creativity. I remember reading that he sometimes used an alarm clock that went off every 10 minutes through the night when he was under time pressure to finish a song for a Broadway show.

I have not yet used that alarm clock trick to write my songs, but on the other hand, if I ever had to write a Broadway show tune under time pressure, then, hell yeah, I would try that alarm clock trick!

If you suffer from insomnia, consider doing the following:
- Have a note pad, pen or pencil, and eraser next to wherever you sleep.
- Have your smartphone with its Voice App next to wherever you sleep.
- Don't curse. Instead, relax and wait for the ideas, muse, or whatever to come your way and record or write them down.

For me, the Voice Memos App on my iPhone is the best tool for recording and remembering my musical and lyrical ideas that may hit me fast and furious. At this very moment, which happens to be 2:45 AM on March 21, 2024, I'm using a mechanical pencil and a pink eraser (like we used in elementary school) to write this chapter. This project has not been a meteoric act of creativity like the writing and composing of some of my songs, but rather a calm and fulfilling experience. It is bringing me much satisfaction knowing that I might be helping my fellow insomniacs feel a little better about their failure to get as much sleep as they feel they need and accepting it as an opportunity for creativity.

It's now 2:58 AM on March 21, 2024. I feel tired and am hopeful that I will get at least a little more sleep—and I feel happy.

CHAPTER 8

IRVING BERLIN'S NINE RULES FOR WRITING POPULAR SONGS

THE BOOK, *As Thousands Cheer (The Life of Irving Berlin)*, by Laurence Bergreen, includes a summary of Irving Berlin's nine rules for writing popular songs, which are:

1. The melody should be within the range of most singers.
2. The title should be attention-getting and, in addition, repeated within the body of the song.
3. The song should be "sexless," able to be sung by men and women.
4. The song requires "heart interest."
5. And at the same time, it should be "original in idea, words, and music."

6. "Stick to nature," advised Berlin in his pragmatic way. "Not nature in a visionary, abstract way, but nature as demonstrated in homely, concrete, everyday manifestations."
7. Sprinkle the lyrics with "open vowels" so that it will be euphonious.
8. Make the song as simple as possible.
9. "The songwriter must look upon his work as a business, that is, to make a success of it, he must work and *work*, and then WORK."

Irving Berlin was arguably the most popular and most commercially successful songwriter of his era, having composed about 1,500 songs of which twenty-five became number one hits. His hits included "Alexander's Ragtime Band," "Always," "Cheek to Cheek," "God Bless America," "White Christmas," and "Easter Parade." He also wrote the songs for the musical *Annie Get Your Gun*.

The business of songwriting today is very different from what it was in Irving Berlin's time. Also, there are no hard and fast rules for writing songs. Many great songs have been written that do not follow Irving Berlin's nine rules. However, his nine rules make good common sense.

Not always, but most of the time when I have deviated from Irving Berlin's nine rules and subsequently revised the song to make it consistent with his rules, the song was better than before.

CHAPTER 9

SONGWRITERS ON SONGWRITING

SIXTY-TWO FAMOUS SONGWRITERS ARE interviewed in *Songwriters on Songwriting (Expanded Fourth Edition)* by Paul Zollo. Below are some of the remarks made by a few of these songwriters.

Pete Seeger mentions that "when you're dozing, that's when the creative ideas come," and "a number of my ideas come early in the morning or late at night…when the brain is somehow released from the pressures of the day."

Paul Simon likes to toss a ball against a wall and catch it while writing songs. He says doing that has a "calming" effect so his "mind will wander." This, in turn, enables him "to pick up words and phrases, fool around with them and drop them." Paul is not interested in writing something he thought about, but rather discovering where his mind wants to go. When Paul writes songs, he wants to think less and feel more.

Paul Simon also said that he believes his songs come from "the river of his subconscious" that can be "magical," that he "doesn't possess it, but rather it comes through him, like he's a transmitter, that he doesn't control or dictate it, but just waits for the show to begin."

During Carol King's interview, she said that "You've Got a Friend" wrote itself, it was pure inspiration written by something outside of her and through her. When she tries to write a song and is getting nowhere, she gets up and does something else and comes back to it. Once the song is coming through her, she works hard at writing it. Also, she likes her songs to be unpredictable by letting the middle of the song go wherever it wants to go. The song has a beginning (home), an unpredictable middle, and an ending in which she brings the song back home where it feels resolved. Carol also believes that "the marriage of the music to the lyrics is key."

Jimmy Webb believes that starting the song with a good title to organize his work around, helps the whole song to stay more focused, and that he "almost has to do it that way." What he also needs when starting a song is to have a chord structure that is inspiring and reasonably original. If he doesn't come up with such a chord structure early on, he does not continue to write the song. He starts out with a title and the chord structure before he writes the melody or words. He describes this chord structure as "sequencing" the chords, "stringing them together like pearls on a string." He finds that "interesting chord sequences will compel interesting melodies."

Jimmy Webb also believes his ideas come from God, and that God is "the author of all this stuff." He also believes that what helps him write songs is to do a lot of other things like painting with watercolors, flying a plane, playing tennis, etc., which acts like a brain scrub—washing out the old notes and chord patterns that are hanging around, so he can come up with new ones.

When Neil Young writes a song, he keeps going until he starts to think, and when he starts to think, he quits. Then, when an idea comes to him out of nowhere, he starts writing the song again. When the ideas stop, he stops. The key for Neil is not to force it when writing a song. When asked where his ideas come from, Neil says he does not know, that it's a mystery to him.

Neil first recognizes that he has an idea for a song and hears a melody for it, over and over again in his head. When that happens, he proceeds with writing the song. When this doesn't happen, he does something else like mowing the lawn.

Paul Zollo says in the Preface of *Songwriters on Songwriting* that "writing a song is genuine magic, miraculous even to those making the miracles." He quotes Bob Dylan as saying, "There's no rhyme or reason to it. There's no rule." He quotes Pete Seeger as saying, "All songwriters are like links in a chain." Paul Zollo explains that "songwriters are forever united in this delicate balancing act of discovering words that seamlessly match the mandate of the music, and music that enhances that lyric with a sense of resonance and organic grace."

What I find most profound is the following that appears in the Preface of Paul Zollo's book:

> *"For songwriting is more than a craft. It's a conscious attempt to connect with the unconscious; a reading beyond ordinary perceptions to grasp images that resonate like dreams, and melodies that haunt and spur the heart. Many songwriters said that their greatest songs were written in a flash, words and music arriving simultaneously, like uncovering something that was already there. Even those that scoffed at the suggestion of a spiritual source of songs admitted that the process is mysterious and can't be controlled . . . one truth remains constant: the writing of a song is a sublime achievement, a triumph of the spirit."*

CHAPTER 10

THE THRILL OF VICTORY AND THE AGONY OF DEFEAT

THOSE WHO ARE BABY boomers, may know that the title of this chapter is not my creation, but that of someone connected with the sports-related TV show in the 1960s *The Wide World of Sports.*

The events described in this chapter really happened to me. I share this to help the songwriter, who might have a similar experience, know that he/she is not alone and can survive the agony of defeat resulting from rejection. You just might end up in a good place like I did, and like the main character in the historical novel *Jean-Christophe* did, which is the subject of Chapter 14 of this book.

The "recording star" and "the intermediary" are not identified herein. That is because "the intermediary" is a dear friend of mine and prefers that I keep him and the recording star anonymous.

In or about late 2014, I told the intermediary that besides golf, I do another activity that I enjoy—songwriting. Then, knowing that the intermediary is a very good and successful business networker, I asked him if he knew any music publishers. He did not know what a music publisher was, so I explained that such a publisher is like a song broker, and when he/she successfully gets a star to record a song, the publisher and songwriter each receive a royalty.

The intermediary said he did not know any music publishers but he knew Nashville stars. I was stunned because this intermediary is a New Yorker, not involved in the music industry, and I was very surprised that he personally knew any Nashville stars. (By the way, country music is not my favorite genre of music—I do not like most modern country music, but do like older classic country music, like that of Johnny Cash, Dolly Parton, etc.) So, I asked the intermediary if he knew the equivalent of today's Johnny Cash? My friend replied that he did!

I asked my friend if he would give my professionally produced first CD containing twelve of my original songs to the recording star so the star could listen to it and consider recording any of the songs on it. The intermediary said sure.

My friend asked the recording star if he/she was interested in receiving "any creative input." The recording star immediately understood what that meant and asked the intermediary if he knew a songwriter. The intermediary replied that he did.

The star listened to my CD, and told the intermediary to "Tell Arnold that the songs on his CD are a great start, but ask him to write a song with a more complex song structure"—like one of the recording star's prior hits that will remain unidentified in this book.

When I learned about the above dialogue, I was highly motivated, and shortly thereafter, began writing a song for the star that used the requested complex song structure.

I was unfamiliar with the recording star's hits, and also unfamiliar with the star himself/herself. So, I Googled the star, read all about him/her, and took notes. I soon came up with what I thought, at the time, was great subject matter and a title for an original song that I was confident I could write because the subject matter happens to be one of my other passions.

Then I wrote the song fast and furious.

I shared it with Kinny Landrum, who is my brilliant arranger, synthesizer, and studio keyboard player, and who has the knowledge and skills to turn my melodies and lyrics into works of art.

I needed some additional creative input from Kinny in order to "finish the hat" because I did not know what a "climb" was (which the Nashville star wanted in the song). So, Kinny explained to me what a climb was, and he wrote the two lines of music that comprised the climb or pre-chorus section of the music in the song. In essence, the climb, musically and lyrically, creates anticipation and tension that gets resolved in the chorus.

Next, was the thrill of victory that Kinny and I came so close to experiencing. The recording star clearly liked the song because when the intermediary, on several occasions over the next three years, ever so gently broached the subject of my song with the recording star, the star replied each time, "50-50 chance I'll record Arnold's song."

Music to my ears, again!

Being an entrepreneur at heart, I went into overdrive writing more songs, which Kinny Landrum professionally arranged, recorded, and produced.

Unfortunately for me, after the star told the intermediary for three years that there was a 50-50 chance he/she would record the song, the star passed on it.

On a PBS special, Judy Collins, in her 70's at that time, said that she is a working girl doing 200 plus public performances per year, and that "the music business will break your heart."

Immediately after I experienced the agony of defeat, I watched my favorite movie, *Field of Dreams*, and gave up songwriting for a full year. During that year, I resumed an old hobby of mine—model railroading—and got hooked on the model railroad I built in my basement as well as the O Gauge Railroad Magazine On-line Forum. These model railroad activities served as another creative outlet and were the perfect medicine for my soul at that time.

Before learning that the recording star passed on my song, the *Field of Dreams* movie inspired me to write an autobiographical song, "Have a Catch with Me," sung by Kinny Landrum.

I've become philosophical about this "thrill of victory and agony of defeat" experience. There were so many amazing coincidences, including meeting someone like Kinny Landrum with his musical expertise. I met him because in 2012 Shawn saw an ad on the Internet about a songwriting class offered by the Hudson Valley Writer's Center—Kinny was the instructor, and I signed up for the class. The coincidences of having a friend from New York, who just happened to have a relationship with a Nashville recording star, and my dreaming up a song for the recording star that seemed to be a perfect fit for him/her made me believe for three years that he/she would record it and that it would be a hit. However, all of those amazing coincidences were thwarted by the free will of that recording star. Whatever, if anything, causes such amazing coincidences to happen, each of us has free will, including the person (in this case the recording star) that may have the power to make the determinative final decision.

CHAPTER 11

JUMPIN' UP AND DOWN EXCITED

AS BRIEFLY MENTIONED EARLIER, the expression "Jumpin' Up and Down Excited" occurred to me when I was tired and about to fall asleep.

My childhood sports hero was Mickey Mantle, Hall of Fame center fielder of the New York Yankees. What came to mind was "The Mick" hitting a World Series walk-off home run, trotting around the bases, and then greeting his teammates at home plate where they were jumping up and down excited. I quickly wrote the lyrics for this first verse about Mickey.

Where the music comes from is largely a mystery for me. With this song, I played some chords on guitar, figured that the song should be up tempo, especially in the chorus that includes the title, and proceeded to hum possible melodies and rhythms into the voice recorder on my smartphone. The music for the first verse also came quickly.

The Evolution of a Most Peculiar Songwriter

Then, I got more ideas for additional verses about *Rocky*, and the 1980 Winter Olympics hockey game in which team USA miraculously defeated the Soviet Union.

Here is my clustering diagram for "Jumpin' Up and Down Excited:"

I ended up composing nine verses for the song that made it about nine minutes long—which is way too long. I've found it best for a song to be three to four minutes long, and not to exceed four and one-half minutes in order to hold the listener's interest.

This reminds me of the great songwriter, Leonard Cohen, who once wrote sixty different verses of lyrics for one of his songs.

A great way to think about those who provide honest feedback about a song is to consider them as part of your songwriting team. In the case of "Jumpin' Up and Down Excited," I got feedback from my wife, Shawn; my daughter, Maria; my music mentor, Kinny Landrum; my friends and music comrades, Rick Tota (Ringo Rick) and Jim Cirrincione; my assistant at my law office, Carol Simon; and audiences at Open Mics.

What can be challenging is making final decisions after getting feedback as to whether to make modifications and, if so, what modifications to make.

The specific feedback I got about "Jumpin' Up and Down Excited," which was so helpful, included the following:

1. Shawn reminded me how excited our granddaughter was when she first learned how to walk. She was beside herself, ecstatic, when she took her first steps without holding the hands of an adult. So, I wrote a verse about that. Here it is:

    Been blessed to see my grandchild learn to walk (4 beats), I was there when she began to crawl.
    Later she stood up and took some steps (2 beats), holding hands, she let go, but many times would fall.
    Then, oh, the magic moment happened (4 beats), she, was, walkin by herself, ecstatic.
    She was walkin, walkin by herself, excited (4 beats), walkin, walkin by herself exci-t-ed (extra bar).

2. Shawn also recommended that I include a verse or two about someone excited about what they do, which is a menial, and not a glamorous, activity. So, I wrote a verse about two mentally challenged busboys who got excited about putting

out the butter and setting the tables at a restaurant where I worked as a busboy when I was a teenager. I wrote another verse about the physically and mentally challenged woman who gets excited about bagging my groceries at a local supermarket. Below are the verses I wrote about the busboys and the grocery bagger:

First, the busboys:

> *Tell you about the busboys at the Grill, the Red Coach Grill in Yonkers years ago.*
> *The challenged busboys got a special thrill, working at the restaurant, where they earned some dough.*
> *Gleefully they placed the pats of butter, the knives and forks and set the dinner tables.*
> *They were jumpin, jumpin up and down excited, jumpin, jumpin up and down exci-t-ed.*

Here is the verse about the grocery bagger:

> *A disabled woman bags my groceries, at a supermarket near my home.*
> *No one loves her jo-b more than her, and does it with more gusto, than God has ever known.*
> *When she bags my groceries I thank her, and sense her pride and feelings of euphoria.*
> *Inside she's jumpin, jumpin up and down excited, jumpin, jumpin up and down, exci-t-ed.*

3. When my daughter, Maria, heard a prior version of the song that included the grocery bagger, she suggested that

I substitute for that verse, another verse about a Special Olympics athlete. So, I Googled Special Olympics athletes and learned about Loretta Claiborne, who was an inspiring Special Olympics runner, figure skater, and bowler, and I wrote a verse about her:

Loretta Claiborne steps up to the line, the five-kilometer race is about to start.
Partially blind, learning disabled too, she will do her best and run the race with all her heart.
Loretta is a Special Olympics athlete, a runner, figure skater, and a bowler.
Whenever she competes, she's excited, jumpin, jumpin up and down exci-t-ed.

4. I even wrote a verse about the excitement I experience as a songwriter:

I started writing songs many years ago, during a sunrise along the Jersey shore.
Pink and mauve aglow in the sea and sky. Then I heard, from deep within, a melody glory born.
Wonder where the words and music come from, all I know is when creation happens.
I am jumpin, jumpin up and down excited, jumpin, jumpin up and down, exci-t-ed.

5. When I played a prior version of the song for my friend, Jim Cirrincione, he recommended that I only include verses about famous athletes, so the song has more commercial appeal.

6. When I played the song for my friend, Rick Tota, he said the verse about Rocky Balboa sent chills up his spine. I was considering omitting that verse to shorten the song but decided to keep the Rocky verse in the song after Rick's positive reaction to it.

7. When I played the song for my music mentor, Kinny Landrum, he recommended that I change a few notes, so the song does not have too wide a vocal range and is easier to sing.

8. My law office assistant, Carol Simon, liked all the verses of the song. (Perhaps that's because I pay her to work as my paralegal.)

9. I also got valuable feedback from performing the song at four different Open Mics. It was evident from the audiences' reactions that the verses about the athletes were most popular. Shawn recommended that I focus the song on athletes by omitting the verse about our granddaughter learning to walk even though it was Shawn's idea to have that verse in the song. So, I deleted that verse, but added a verse about my granddaughter's cheerleading, a sport most commonly done by girls and women. Now, the song not only focuses on athletes, but is also inclusive of both genders. Here is a photo of my granddaughter (Maria's daughter) performing as a cheerleader flyer.

The hardest verse for me to cut was the one about my granddaughter (also Maria's daughter) learning to walk, which I loved, but there's no question in my mind that the song will have the most commercial and universal appeal by limiting it to about four and one-half minutes in length and having it focused on athletes and sporting events.

Based on how the audiences responded, I also changed the ending of the song. Originally, the lyrics for the refrain at the end said that we can all be excited about whatever we do. That is a nice sentiment, but I believe the final version of the ending is better because it simply repeats the refrain with the musical and lyrical hook about how excited my daughter, Maria, feels when she sees her daughter flying through the air as a cheerleader flyer.

"Jumpin' Up and Down Excited" is sung by Maria Cribari, and here is a photo of Maria.

The final lyrics that Maria sings are as follows:

Jumpin' Up and Down Excited
© 2024 Arnold D. Cribari

Mickey Mantle steps up to home plate (4 beats), waggles the bat with the game on the line.
The wind up begins and here comes the pitch (2 beats). Mickey swings, there it goes, a home run so sublime.
The Mick hits a Wo-rld Series walk-off (4 beats), and gree-ts his teammates at home plate.
They are jumpin', jumpin' up and down excited (4 beats), jumpin', jumpin' up and down, exci-t-ed (extra bar).

Rocky goes the distance in the fight (4 beats), he is bruised and bloody in the end.
So - is the great Apollo Creed (2 beats), punches thrown, both go down, the countdown's close to ten.
Rocky rises Apollo Creed collapses (4 beats), the Italian Stallion shouts: "Yo Adrienne I did it!"
There is jumpin', jumpin' up and down, excitement (4 beats); jumpin', jumpin' up and down exci-t-ement. (extra bar).

The 1980 Winter Olympic Games (4 beats), the Soviets facing off with the USA.
The blades of their skates slice through the ice (2 beats). Score is tied, Eruzione shoots - Hooray!
Michaels makes the call: Do you believe in miracles - Yes, Team USA wins the game.
They are jumpin', huggin' on the ice, excited (4 beats), jumpin', huggin' on the ice exci-t-ed (extra bar).

Jumpin' Up and Down Excited

My daughter is an athlete who has done (4 beats), a jumpin' up and down sport for years.
As pop and hip-hop music blares away (2 beats), she shouts out, with her team, the coolest kick-ass cheers.
Standing on, another cheerleader's shoulders (4 beats), then jumpin', jumpin' in the ai-r fly-ing.
She's a flyer, flying in the air, excited (4 beats), flying, flying in the air, exci-t-ed. [No extra bar]

When I see my cheerleader daughter (4 beats), flying through the air I get excited.
Jumpin', jumpin' up and down, exci-t-ed; jumpin', jumpin' up and down excited;
Jumpin', jumpin' up and down, exci-t-ed.

I believe that the subject matter, title, and musical hook in the refrain of "Jumpin' Up and Down Excited" is such that it might have the potential to be a hit. Recently, while I performed it at an open mic, a stranger in the audience shouted a cheer when I sang the third verse about Team USA defeating the Soviet Union's ice hockey team in the 1980 Winter Olympics. That's the kind of reaction that's music to the ears of a songwriter like me.

This contrasts with my song discussed in the next chapter, "Cinderella's Eyes" formerly known as "Rings of Saturn," which I think has little, if any, hit potential, and I regard as an art song.

In October 2024, I revisited the lyrics in "Jumpin' Up and Down Excited," specifically the first verse about Mickey Mantle, the Hall of Fame baseball player who was my childhood hero (he was also Paul Simon's childhood hero). I was motivated to do this because the New York Yankees made it to the 2024 World Series and have a great, future Hall of Famer named Aaron Judge; and the

Mets, who made amazing come backs to get into the 2024 playoffs and win numerous playoff games, have a great slugger, Pete Alonso.

I had a great time writing new first verses about Aaron Judge and Pete Alonso. This enables me to ask my New York audiences whether they are mostly Mets fans or mostly Yankee fans, before I perform "Jumpin' Up and Down Excited."

If they are Mets fans, I sing the following lyrics about Pete Alonzo:

> *Pete Alonzo steps up to home plate, waggles the bat with the game on the line.*
> *The wind up begins and here comes the pitch. Alonzo swings, there it goes, a homerun so sublime.*
> *The polar bear hits a play-off walk-off and greets his teammates at home plate.*
> *They are jumpin', jumpin' up and down excited, jumpin', jumpin' up and down excited.*

If my New York audience is mostly Yankee fans, I can sing the original Mickey Mantle first verse (especially if my audience is mostly old-timers like me), or I can sing my new Aaron Judge first verse:

> *Aaron Judge steps up to home plate, waggles the bat with the game on the line.*
> *The wind up begins and here comes the pitch. Aaron swings, there it goes, a homerun so sublime.*
> *The Yankee captain hits a play-off walk-off and greets his teammates at home plate.*
> *They are jumpin', jumpin' up and down excited, jumpin', jumpin' up and down excited.*

CHAPTER 12

RINGS OF SATURN/ CINDERELLA'S EYES

IN **FEBRUARY 2024, SHORTLY** before I wrote "Jumpin' Up and Down Excited," I wrote "Rings of Saturn," now with the new title "Cinderella's Eyes."

Writing this song began when I watched an episode of my favorite TV show about astronomy *How the Universe Works*. At the beginning of this episode, a college professor in Astrophysics, who was very passionate about astronomy, said that when she was five years old, she saw the planet Saturn through a telescope and thought it was so beautiful that she decided after that to become an astrophysicist.

The thought occurred to me that the beauty of the rings of Saturn could be comparable to the ethereal eyes of a beautiful young woman. I had seen beautiful ethereal blue gray eyes when I was seventeen years old and fell in love with a pretty fifteen-year-old girl who had such eyes.

Below is my initial cluster of lyrics for "Rings of Saturn," and beneath that is the first version of the title and lyrics of the song:

The Evolution of a Most Peculiar Songwriter

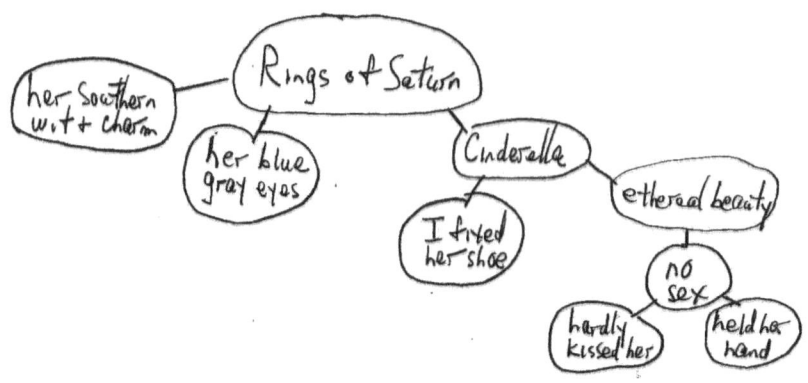

Rings of Saturn
© Arnold D. Cribari 2024

It's crazy maybe dangerous, for me to write this song,
Of ancient, unrequited love, I should think of her no more.
The only good that may come of this is a kind of therapy,
What I risk is once again, to be wounded to the core.

I first saw my ethereal princess clad in a white prom dress,
We met with friends and family at a country barbeque.
I asked her to take a walk with me, she smiled approvingly,
As we walked, she stumbled when the heel broke off
  her shoe.

Then the mi-ra-cle happened, barefoot she walked with me
  on the farm into a barn.
I found a hammer there —though I'm no good with tools,
  while in the barn
Somehow someway I fixed her broken shoe, Cinderella's
  broken shoe —

*And I gazed into her eyes, Cinderella's eyes, ethereal
    and beautiful,*
*I saw the rings of Saturn there—the beauty of the rings of
    Saturn the-r-e.*

Lovestruck after that I took Cinderella to Broadway shows.
She was always home by midnight that was guaranteed.
*She loved the Beatles, I, The Doors, we romped through the
    Bro-nx Zoo.*
*When our friendship ended, how my broken heart
    did bleed.*

Songwriters like me are known to play with the fire of love.
*Luckily like Saturn she's a billion miles away, a billion
    miles away, in time and space.*
If I get too close to her, a black hole beckons me,
This song is done so now a billion miles away I'll stay.
I will stay in time and space a billion miles away.
But I'm still haunted by the rings of Saturn in her eyes.

You can hear me sing the final version of this song, now entitled "Cinderella's Eyes," by accessing it using the QR Code for it, or by going on a music platform like Spotify, Apple Music, iTunes, etc., and searching for it under my name.

I considered modifying the music of "Rings of Saturn" because it's unusual and the chords lack resolution. However, I decided that I wanted the song to evoke unresolved feelings, which are even expressed in the first line of lyrics, "It's crazy maybe dangerous for me to write this song."

After reflecting on the music of "Rings of Saturn" for a few days, I came to the conclusion that the music correctly expressed what I wanted the song to say, and that it was not only aesthetically pleasing, at least to me, but also original, so I decided not to change it.

The music that is most unusual and original is in the middle of the song.

As Carole King said during her interview in Paul Zollo's book, *Songwriters on Songwriting*, which is the subject of Chapter 9, she likes to be unpredictable, and goes wherever the music takes her in the middle of her songs. I believe I did the same thing with the music in the middle of "Rings of Saturn" (now "Cinderella's Eyes").

It occurred to me that the title I loved, "Rings of Saturn," might be one of my "darlings" that needed to be changed. I discussed this with Shawn, and she agreed that Rings of Saturn did not quite work as a metaphor for the beautiful eyes of a young woman, so I decided to modify the title and lyrics.

My "darling" Rings of Saturn is a forced metaphor. Are the eyes of a pretty girl fully comparable to the rings of the planet, Saturn, in our solar system? I don't think so.

What initially confused me were the thoughts that the irises of the eyes have rings, and the beautiful eyes of a pretty teenage girl can have an ethereal quality like the rings of Saturn. However, notwithstanding these thoughts—which have some merit—the girl's eyes are not like the rings of Saturn in all respects.

So I changed the title of the song to "Cinderella's Eyes" and changed other lyrics as shown by the following lyric sheet:

Cinderella's Eyes
© Arnold D. Cribari 2024

It's crazy maybe dangerous, for me to write this song,
Of ancient, unrequited love, I should think of her no more.
The only good that may come of this is a kind of therapy,
What I risk is, once again, to be wounded to the core.

I first saw my ethereal princess clad in a white prom dress.
We met with friends and family at a country barbeque.
I asked her to take a walk with me, she smiled approvingly,
As we walked, she stumbled when the heel broke off
   her shoe.

Then the mi-ra-cle happened, barefoot she walked with me
   on the farm into a barn,
I found a hammer there —though I'm no good with tools,
   while in the barn
Somehow someway I fixed her broken shoe, Cinderella's
   broken shoe.

And I gazed into her eyes, Cinderella's eyes, ethereal
   and beautiful,
Cinderella's blue gray e-y-es, Cinderella's blue gray e-y-e-s.

Lovestruck after that I took Cinderella to Broadway shows,
She was always home by midnight that was guaranteed.
She loved the Beatles, I, The Doors, we romped through the
   Bro-nx Zoo.
When our friendship ended, how my broken heart
   did bleed.

Songwriters like me are known to play with the fire of love.
Luckily like Saturn she's a billion miles away, a billion miles away, in time and space,
If I get too close to her, a black hole beckons me.
This song is done so now a billion miles away I'll stay.
I will stay in time and space a billion miles away.
But I'm still haunted by the ethereal beauty of her eyes.

On the evening of May 23rd, 2024, I performed both, "Cinderella's Eyes" and "Jumpin' Up and Down Excited," at an Open Mic after asking several people in advance to give me their honest feedback. To my surprise, they preferred "Cinderella's Eyes" over "Jumpin' Up and Down Excited."

This surprised me because I thought "Jumpin' Up and Down Excited" had more mass appeal because it's upbeat and has three verses about iconic athletes and sports events, whereas "Cinderella's Eyes" is a bittersweet love song about a young love that ended up unrequited—and I think its music and lyrics are very unusual.

However, the title and lyric "Cinderella's Eyes," is a metaphor that fully works in the song. That is because in the story of the song, the teenage girl has qualities in common with Cinderella. She has a problem with her shoe, which was fixed by me—making me feel like a Prince (Cinderella lost her glass slipper that was found by the Prince), she is first seen by the singer wearing a white prom dress (Cinderella goes to the ball in a beautiful (probably white) gown, and both are beautiful young women that must be home by midnight.

I believe my re-write of "Rings of Saturn," changing it to "Cinderella's Eyes," substantially improved the song.

On May 29, 2024, my daughter, Maria, and I met with Kinny Landrum at his basement recording studio for Maria to do a vocal track for "Jumpin' Up and Down Excited." It was a peak experience for me to witness Maria sing that vocal track beautifully with Kinny's skillful coaching.

After that vocal track was completed, I performed "Cinderella's Eyes" for Kinny and Maria. As usual, Kinny's critique was extremely helpful. He said that the title, "Cinderella's Eyes" was excellent, and I should repeat it more often throughout the song. Repeating a good title is the second of Irving Berlin's nine rules for writing popular songs, so I immediately knew Kinny's recommendation had merit.

Kinny made several other recommendations for modifications, which I made, including having another bridge section (the music in the bridge is passionate and appears in the middle of the song), so I composed an additional bridge just before the final verse.

On June 5, 2024, Shawn recommended that I have another astronomical term at the beginning of the song to set up the references to "Saturn" and "black hole" mentioned in the last verse, so I changed the second line in the first verse to say, "She used to be the center of the universe for me…"

Below is the lyric sheet for the final draft of the song:

Cinderella's Eyes
© Arnold D. Cribari 2024

It's crazy maybe dangerous, for me to write this song, of ancient, unrequited love, I should think of her no more. She used to be the center of the universe for me, what I risk is, once again, to be wounded to the core.

I first saw my ethereal princess clad in a white prom dress, we met with friends and family at a country barbeque.

The Evolution of a Most Peculiar Songwriter

*I asked her to take a walk with me, she smiled approvingly,
as we walked, she stumbled when the heel broke off
her shoe.*

*Then the mi-ra-cle happened, barefoot she walked with me
on the farm into a barn.
I found a hammer there —and with the hammer in
the barn.
I fixed her broken shoe, Cinderella's broken shoe —*

*I gazed into her eyes, Cinderella's eyes, ethereal
and beautiful,
Cinderella's blue gray eyes, Cinderella's blue gray e-y-e-s-*

*Lovestruck after that I took Cinderella to Broadway shows,
she was always home by midnight that was guaranteed.
She loved the Beatles, I, The Doors, we sang their songs
too, when our friendship ended, how my broken heart
did bleed.*

*I wanted Cinderella, to let me be her Prince, but she
wanted another Prince: handsome George Harr-i-so-n
Woe oh woe was me, homely, homely me, Cinderella's
eyes for me, became a memory, Cinderella's eyes for me,
became a memory.*

*Songwriters like me are known to play with the fire of love,
luckily like Saturn she's a billion miles away.
If I get too close to her, a black hole beckons me,
This song is done, so now a billion miles away I'll stay, but
I'm still haunted by the beauty of Cinderella's eyes.*

I love the ending of "Cinderella's Eyes," which includes a hyperbole and a metaphor. In the ending I say that the beloved is a billion miles away from me like the planet Saturn. This is metaphorically true because the real girl, now a 70-year-old woman, is married to another man and lives in New Hampshire which, for me, makes her the equivalent of being a billion miles away since I'm married to another woman and live far away in a suburb of New York City. I also acknowledge in the ending that I will continue to stay a billion miles away from her, which is good for me emotionally. However, to add a little drama, I say that I'm still haunted by the beauty of Cinderella's eyes.

Now, the song is not only bittersweet, involving unrequited love, but also humorous. I added truthful lyrics that my Cinderella had a crush on George Harrison of The Beatles, who, of course, was impossible for me to compete with. Compared to handsome George Harrison, I truly felt homely, even though I know I'm not a bad looking fellow, and this rejection of me intensified my feelings for her all the more, causing me to miss the beauty of Cinderella's eyes. I think the addition of this humor involving teenage puppy love, makes this otherwise bittersweet song more entertaining. I also think that many can relate to it when reminiscing about their own first loves.

I share these re-writes to demonstrate the potential of improving songs by re-writing and modifying them. This is not always necessary, but I have found that most of my songs were improved by making such re-writes and modifications—sometimes over a period of years.

I also think that audiences have responded positively to this song because of its originality and because it has a universal theme—it's not uncommon to fall victim to unrequited love, like I did as a teenager when I fell for my Cinderella, and Cinderella is a cherished literary character and story.

One more thing, it turned out to be very good therapy for me to write the song. My teenage beloved was a charming and beautiful girl, but I now know that I loved the idea of Cinderella just as much, if not more, than the actual girl.

I plan to continue to perform it at future Open Mics and gigs, and I can't wait to get feedback from the audiences.

CHAPTER 13

DIFFERENT GENRES OF MUSIC AND MISCELLANEOUS SONGS

BY COMPOSING IN DIFFERENT genres of music, like I have, you can pick the genre that you believe works best for the song. When asked what my genre of music is, I say "eclectic."

ROCK N' ROLL

Being a teenager in the mid and late 1960's, I was heavily influenced by the music of that era and my favorite groups and recording artists were The Beatles, Simon & Garfunkel, Bob Dylan, and especially The Doors.

Four of my original songs are rock n' roll.

"Lovin' Darlin'" and "My Harem" are both sung by Lou Del Bianco, shown in the photo on the next page. These rock n' roll songs are musically reminiscent of The Doors.

Another original rock n' roll song of mine is "Icing on the Cake," sung by my daughter, Maria Cribari, and me. While we were recording "Icing on the Cake" in Kinny Landrum's basement recording studio, Maria had a hard time keeping from laughing because I was so "into it" and Kinny said he thought we sounded like Sonny and Cher. It was a peak experience for me to sing that song with my daughter, Maria.

"Uber Driven Hard Drivin' Man" is a rock n' roll song written by me and a friend of mine, Don Solomon, and is sung by Don. Don was working as an Uber driver at the time.

COUNTRY

Another song I wrote for the Nashville recording star discussed in Chapter 10 is: "Bad Ole Boy." I sing it and it is in the style of classic country music.

The title, "Bad Ole Boy," is an example of how you can take a cliché such as, "good ole boy," and give it a twist to make the title and the song more interesting.

Other country music songs of mine are "Whiskey and a Woman So Fine," "Down by the Reservoir," "Have a Catch with Me," and "Collaborative Country Lawyer."

LOVE SONGS

When I first shared my song, "The Stars We See Tonight," with Kinny Landrum, he said he wouldn't change a note or a word of it, which is a high compliment coming from him. Richard Lindsey, a studio guitarist who did the guitar track for that song, gave me a similar compliment when he told me that it was a really good song.

When my daughter, Maria, was a little girl, she followed her mother, Shawn, around. Remembering this inspired me to write "My Shadow." In the recording, Maria sings "My Shadow" as an adult and the mother of her own daughters.

A song in the style of a Broadway show tune is "Collaborate with Me," which is another love song of mine that I sing.

Collaboration also relates to my work as a collaborative divorce lawyer, and I have written a song about that mentioned later in this chapter.

"Au Revoir My Friend" is a love song inspired by *Andre's Mother*, a television show I saw on American Playhouse. When I wrote that song, I imagined what it would be like to be one of the main characters in *Andre's Mother*, who was a gay man from New York City that lost his talented lover to AIDS. The lyrics have expressions I imagine the surviving gay man, mourning his loss, would say, such as, "We climbed the Eiffel Tower, in New York City restaurants, over coffee, conversation and your smile" and "Like Mozart you made music, turning life into perfection, and before the age of forty you were free." In the bridge of the song, the surviving gay man expresses his anger, "Free from the virus that took you from me, I was lost and alone, feeling anger and grief."

Interestingly, the song doesn't mention AIDS and could be about a heterosexual couple stricken by the Coronavirus in which the survivor expresses his/her loss.

"Au Revoir My Friend" is sung by Maria Cribari.

CHRISTIAN & SPIRITUAL SONGS

In addition to "Earthrise" and "Oh Good Earth," I have another spiritual music video, "The Deck," that you can access on YouTube under my name. Here is a photo of Maria and Shawn singing on the deck of our home at our annual Open Mic barbecue:

"Painting the Stars," an adult-ed program my wife and I attended at our church, inspired me to write "The Deck." (The study, "Painting the Stars," was inspired by a quote from Vincent van Gogh, "When I have a terrible need of, shall I say the word—religion, then I go out and paint the stars.")

Thirty years ago, my wife and I went on a midnight run in New York City with members of our church. During the midnight run, we handed out food and clothing to homeless people. This experience inspired me to write "Prayer for the Homeless," a Christian song sung by Maria Cribari.

"You are Unique" is another Christian/spiritual song. It is written by me, sung by Maria Cribari, and the music has a medieval quality.

After we attended a Church adult-ed program about the Book of Job in the Old Testament, I was inspired to write "The Man from Uz," sung by Maria Cribari.

HUMOR

One cannot go wrong with writing songs that are humorous, put a smile on the faces of those in the audience, and get them to laugh. I know this from going to many Open Mics over the past 10 years.

"My Ravishing Russian Spy" is a James Bond spoof song, co-written by Kinny Landrum (music) and me (lyrics) and sung by Lou Del Bianco.

Sally was our family pet, a German Shepherd-Beagle mix. She became the subject of a humorous song, "Ode to Sally," sung by me.

Ken Burns has a film series on the history of baseball that includes the 1970's era in which the Hall of Fame pitcher, Catfish Hunter, is interviewed after he had a less than stellar game. During that interview, when Catfish was asked why he had an off day he said, "Well, the sun don't shine on the same dog's ass every day." When I heard that, I had to write a song about it. The title of this song is "What Did Catfish Say?" It was co-written by Kinny Landrum (music) and me (lyrics) and is sung by me.

NOVELTY SONGS

"Who Am I (Rollin' By)" about model railroading is a novelty song mentioned in Chapter 1. You can hear it, sung by me, on YouTube under my name as part of my music video with the same title.

Another novelty song is a mostly autobiographical song about my Martin guitar. When I was 15 years old (in 1966), my mother bought me a Martin nylon string guitar. This guitar was identical to the one my older sister, Idaehla, had. Idaehla taught me to play chords on my Martin guitar to accompany my singing, and I have composed most of my songs using it. I treasure that guitar. "My Sweet Martin" is sung by Lou Del Bianco.

"My Sweet Martin" is part fiction and part non-fiction. Sometimes I add some fiction to make a song more interesting. For instance, I say in this song that My Sweet Martin and I went down South, were swindled, got into a fight in a bar and landed in jail. None of that really happened.

Incidentally, when I wrote "My Sweet Martin" the music and lyrics came to me simultaneously and I completed the song in two hours, which was a thrilling experience. I believe some mysterious force wrote it—or helped me write it.

"Dollar Bill" is also a novelty song. Although Dollar Bill is the nickname for Bill Bradley, the former Princeton and New York

Knicks basketball player who also became a US Senator, my song is not about him. Instead, it's about the images on the back of a one-dollar bill—the American bald eagle, what it is holding in its talons, and the pyramid with the eyeball on top. Those images intrigued me, so I wrote "Dollar Bill."

SEA SHANTY

As mentioned earlier, Jimmy Webb's "Highwayman," a song involving reincarnation, inspired me to write my own reincarnation song "Whiskey and a Woman So Fine."

"Highwayman" also inspired me to write another song involving reincarnation "Your Siren Song." When Kinny Landrum heard it and did the arrangement, he changed the rhythm and made it into a sea shanty, which I love.

"Your Siren Song" is sung by me, with my daughter, Maria, singing the "ooos" in the background as the Siren.

CLASSICAL

What astonishes me the most is my song "Jean-Christophe." I believe the music of that song is in the style of classical music. "Jean-Christophe" is the subject of Chapter 14 of this book, which includes the lyrics, and is sung by Lou Del Bianco.

In view of my almost total lack of formal musical education and inability to read music, I truly believe that some mysterious force used me as a conduit to write "Jean-Christophe."

SONGS ABOUT MY WORK

"Collaborative Country Lawyer" is a song I wrote about my work as a collaborative divorce lawyer and mediator. I performed it with a few of my collaborative divorce colleagues before several hundred people in San Francisco at an Annual Conference of the International Academy of Collaborative Professionals. "Collaborative Country Lawyer" is sung by me.

In 2023, I was preparing for trial in one of my Family Law cases. To get myself psyched for going to trial, I wrote a song entitled "Make My Day," in which the singer not only sings, but also howls like a wolf. Keep in mind that my late uncle, Wolfe Cribari, was a legendary trial lawyer in the Westchester County, NY area and is the subject of the book, *Wolfe with an E*, written by his daughter, Camille Cribari Linen, mentioned earlier.

"Make My Day" is sung by Lou Del Bianco.

SONG ABOUT IMMIGRANT GRANDPARENTS

Although I hardly knew my paternal grandparents, Benjamino and Eugenia Cribari, Camille Cribari Linen's book, *Wolfe with an E*, enlightened me with interesting information about them including numerous photographs.

I had started writing a song "The Spirit of America" about my paternal grandparents and their immigrant experience about ten years ago, but in year 2023 when I read *Wolfe with an E*, I revisited the song and re-wrote much of it. The final version of "Spirit of America" is sung by Lou Del Bianco.

POLITICAL

I've admired folk singer/songwriters who have written political songs like Pete Seeger, who wrote "If I Had a Hammer," and Bob Dylan, who wrote "Blowing in the Wind." "Blowing in the Wind" was the first song I learned to play on the guitar when I was a teenager.

President Barack Obama is a political figure that I think is a great man, so much so that I have a six-foot, one inch cardboard President Obama with his arms folded smiling at me at all times in the corner of my living room. (My cardboard President Obama was a gift from my daughter, Maria.) A photo I took of my cardboard President Obama appears below:

"Malala Mandela and Obama" is a political song with a positive message that I have written. It is sung by Lou Del Bianco.

POSSIBLE FUTURE SONGS

The only genres of songs I have not yet written that I can think of, are the blues, hip hop and rap.

I should be able to write a blues song, but hip hop and rap? I don't know about that. I can't help but think that I may be too old to write songs in those genres, but who knows what the future will bring?

CHAPTER 14

JEAN-CHRISTOPHE

AFTER TWO YEARS OF being told that a recording star said there was a 50-50 chance he would record my song, doubts started creeping into my mind that maybe it wouldn't happen.

At that time, I decided to re-read an historical novel I read as a teenager entitled *Jean-Christophe* (John Christopher in English) written by Romain Rolland. *Jean-Christophe* is one of the longest novels ever written, comprises 10 volumes, and won the Nobel Prize for Literature in year 1915.

In essence, the story of *Jean-Christophe* is loosely based on the life of Ludwig Von Beethoven. The main character of the book has many things in common with Beethoven: both were abused children; both had to practice the piano for extremely long hours as a child (Jean-Christophe was made to practice so much that there was not enough time for him to be taught how to eat with a knife and fork during his childhood); the relentless practice paid off to the extent that they both became excellent pianists and, later on, brilliant composers; they both experienced bad cases of unrequited love; they both loved to take long walks in the woods where they often composed music; and they were both strong-willed and physically robust. The main difference between them was that Beethoven was highly celebrated as a composer during his earthly life and his works are arguably eternal, while such was not the case for fictitious Jean Christophe even though his works were just as good as that of Beethoven.

I have written a song entitled "Jean-Christophe" and its lyrics, which tell the essential story of the book, appear below.

JEAN-CHRISTOPHE
© Arnold D. Cribari, 2017

*Crowds applauded Jean-Christophe, a Belgian
  music prodigy.
Now he's hardly known, how can that be?*

*Lacking in the social graces, he was steeped in poverty.
Wouldn't kowtow to nobility.*

*Melodies that he composed, were his sweet bouquet of roses.
They inspired love but not for poor Jean-Christophe.*

*Jean-Christophe was honest and an idealistic,
  truthful man,
Fought hypocrisy and took a stand.*

*Frequently and desperately, he fell in love then fell apart.
Women left him with a broken heart.
Walking through the woods all day, songs would find their
  way to him.
Like soaring eagles landing on the peaks of mountains.*

Jean-Christophe

In the end, Jean-Christophe had won,
When the gossip stopped, and the affairs were done.
Though almost alone, and almost unknown
Rave reviews and Bravos came from those - who -
Deeply moved, heard Heaven, they heard him.

How can such a virtuoso seem forgotten and long gone?
Jean-Christophe is just a dusty novel by Romain Rolland.

So, it is our tragic hero, in a novel isn't real.
But then again, sometimes I feel, oh God - I -feel - like
Jean-Christophe lives in me.

This song, "Jean-Christophe," is written by me, and sung by Lou Del Bianco, a professional actor and singer as well as an author.

The historical novel *Jean-Christophe* is an award-winning book with a profoundly important message. That message is whether or not you achieve financial success or fame, your works, like those of the Jean-Christophe character, may be greatly appreciated by a limited audience in addition to providing fulfillment to you as the creator and, in my opinion, that is wonderful.

Its meaning applies not only to composers, but also to artists (painters, sculptors, writers, actors, singers, musicians, dancers, etc.), athletes, performers, and creative people of all kinds.

My cousin, Camille, in her book, *Wolfe with a E*, and my wife, Shawn, reminded me of the following quote from Kurt Vonnegut:

"Practicing an art, no matter how well or badly, is a way to make your soul grow, for heaven's sake. Sing in the shower. Dance to the radio. Write a poem to a friend, even a lousy

poem. Do it as well as you possibly can. You will get an enormous reward. You will have created something."

CHAPTER 15

CULTIVATE YOUR GARDEN

THE ULTIMATE THEME OF Voltaire's *Candide, ou l'Optisme* has a meaning similar to the message of *Jean-Christophe* described above. That theme in *Candide* is to cultivate your garden. It can be taken literally (planting, growing, and tending to flowers or vegetables) or metaphorically. When taken metaphorically, it's a good way to live one's life, and I embrace it.

Metaphorically, to cultivate my garden means that regardless of how good or bad I may be in doing whatever activities I choose, there is goodness, meaning and enjoyment in doing them (provided that no one gets hurt, and they are intrinsically positive).

Songwriting, a sport, reading a good book, acting (or any creative endeavor), raising a family, teaching, doing an occupation that provides a product or service, or helping others do anything—all of these activities and many others are fulfilling ways for each of us to cultivate our respective gardens.

Cultivating one's garden can help cope with the challenges of life, as well as provide much fulfillment. In my song about model railroading, "Who Am I (Rollin' By)," I have the following line of lyrics in the chorus, "In my little world I leave this troubled world behind." That was so true for me in my career as a divorce litigator when I would go home and get my mind off my stressful work by entering my little world of model trains in my basement.

I got the same psychic relief when I played golf in a golf league from 2001 through 2007. Golf requires a lot of focus and practice for me to be any good at it, and this also helped me cope with my stressful occupation.

Playing golf in the golf league inspired me to write and sing a humorous song about sleeping in a car overnight to get an early tee time for golf entitled "Man of Mohansic," with Kinny Landrum playing the keyboard in the style of the ragtime music that I love.

If we sense that we are getting better at doing the things that comprise our gardens, well, that can be exhilarating.

I hope this book helps you as a songwriter. Songwriting can be a beautiful flower in your garden. It has been exhilarating for me to write this book and to write songs, and I hope that you have similar experiences.

CHAPTER 16

FINAL THOUGHTS

WHEN MY SON, DAVID Cribari, was about 25 years old, he made an astute remark to me about songwriting—that writing songs involves a completely different skill set compared to performing them. I wholeheartedly agree.

There are many singer/songwriters that are highly talented as songwriters and performers. However, there are more artists, like me, who do not excel at both disciplines. When I describe my involvement with music to others, I often say I'm just a nerdy lyricist who can dream up a catchy tune, and I'm, at best, an average singer and guitar player.

From what I've experienced personally and observed, it is much harder to make money and gain recognition as a songwriter than as a performer. Most singers and musicians who get paid for doing gigs, only perform cover songs, not originals. They rarely even perform their own originals at such gigs.

It is also challenging today for a songwriter to find a music publisher or recording artist willing to consider unsolicited submissions.

If you hope to make money exclusively as a songwriter and write a song heard around the world, even assuming you're an outstanding songwriter, I believe the odds are against you to achieve such goals. So, it may be best "not to give up your day job."

Now, as a 72-year-old songwriter, I only write songs when inspired to do so and when musical and lyrical ideas pop into my head. I do it for my own enjoyment and to entertain those willing to listen. I no longer do it for the purpose of making any money.

I consider myself fortunate to earn enough as an attorney to make ends meet, maintain an economically middle-class lifestyle, and still have the occasional exhilarating experience of writing songs and sharing them with others.

Let's say you are like me and consider yourself to be a very good songwriter and mediocre performer. The good news is that there are many outstanding performers out there, and if you can afford to pay them for a few hours of their time, you can turn your songs into works of art by hiring a first-rate singer and musician when your song is recorded. I have done that by hiring my daughter, Maria Cribari, who the recording star mentioned in Chapter 10 said was good enough to be a Nashville back-up singer (paying my daughter is like paying myself), hiring Lou Del Bianco (a professional singer), hiring Kinny Landrum (a studio keyboard player, arranger, synthesizer, producer and recorder), and hiring Richard Lindsey (a studio guitarist). (For those of you who don't know, a studio musician is so highly skilled, that he/she can almost always play any song beautifully on a musical instrument after hearing it only once. It's been amazing for me to witness Kinny Landrum and Richard Lindsey in action doing this.)

Here is a photo of Kinny Landrum:

And here is a photo of Richard Lindsey:

I also want to thank a brilliant young man, Noah Volkman, who I miraculously met in May 2024. Noah is an expert in music technology. He uploaded onto Distrokid and the music platforms all the songs mentioned on the following "List of Songs and QR Codes." I did not even know what a QR Code was until I met Noah. Noah also masterfully created the artwork for those songs and all the QR Codes for them.

Here is a photo of Noah:

A BLAZE OF CREATIVITY

A final thought occurred to me moments after I thought I had finished this book. I thought about how some iconic artists, upon learning that they had a terminal illness, went into overdrive with their creative pursuits.

Although I'm not familiar with his songs, I understand that David Bowie did this when he created his final album, *Blackstar*.

I have the good fortune of being a relatively healthy 72-year-old, but I also know that, like Jim Morrison of The Doors said, "No one gets out of here alive."

In my final days, I hope to go out in a blaze of creativity like David Bowie did.

Finally, I previously mentioned that my musical awakening occurred in the 1960's. I listened to the folk and rock n roll music of that era including The Beatles, Simon and Garfunkel, and Bob Dylan, but my favorite group was The Doors. The Doors made me feel good as a teenage male in the late 1960's/early 1970's.

The music of The Doors filled my soul and never left it. Although none of my songs are identical to any of the songs of The Doors, a few of them have characteristics of The Doors' music, including "Lovin' Darlin'" (especially the rhythm), "My Harem" (especially the intro and its chord progression) and "Uber Drivin' Hard Drivin Man" (the drivin' beat). I consider them to be an homage to The Doors.

With that in mind, Richard Lindsey is my Robbie Krieger, Kinny Landrum is my combination Paul Rothschild (producer), and Ray Manzarek (keyboard player and arranger), Lou Del Bianco, and Maria Cribari are my combination Jim Morrison because they are great lead singers.

A List of Songs with QR Codes begins on the following page. In order to access my songs on the various music platforms like Spotify using the QR Codes, this is how you do it—first, point your smartphone camera at the QR Code without taking the photo; then, you will see a narrow, small rectangular box on the bottom of your screen that says "Distrokid.com;" then, tap on that box. When you do that, you will see various music platforms. If you have a Spotify premium account (that costs about $11.00 per month), tap on Spotify and you can see and hear the whole song. If you don't have a Spotify premium account and only have the free Spotify App, then you will only hear a snippet of the song when you tap on Spotify.

You can also hear the whole song for free by getting a YouTube App for free, inserting my name and the title of my song in the YouTube search box, and tapping on the song.

BONUS

LIST OF SONGS WITH QR CODES

Title	QR Code	Page
Glory Born		8
Down by the Reservoir		16

The Evolution of a Most Peculiar Songwriter

Prayer for the Homeless		16
Whiskey and a Woman So Fine		24
Have a Catch with Me		46
Jumpin' Up and Down Excited		47
Cinderella's Eyes		55

List of Songs with QR Codes

Lovin' Darlin'		67
My Harem		67
Icing on the Cake		68
Uber Driven Hard Drivin' Man		68
Bad Ole Boy		68

The Evolution of a Most Peculiar Songwriter

The Stars We See Tonight		69
My Shadow		69
Collaborate with Me		69
Au Revoir My Friend		69
You are Unique		71

List of Songs with QR Codes

The Man from Uz		71
My Ravishing Russian Spy		71
Ode to Sally		71
What Did Catfish Say?		72
My Sweet Martin		72

The Evolution of a Most Peculiar Songwriter

Song	QR	Page
Dollar Bill		72
Your Siren Song		73
Collaborative Country Lawyer		74
Make My Day		74
The Spirit of America		75

List of Songs with QR Codes

Malala Mandela and Obama		76
Jean-Christophe		77
Man of Mohansic		82

BONUS

LIST OF MUSIC VIDEOS ON YOUTUBE

Music Video	Page
Who Am I (Rollin' By)	1
Earthrise	17
Oh Good Earth	29
The Deck	70

BIBLIOGRAPHY

Bergreen, Laurence. *As Thousands Cheer (The Life of Irving Berlin)*. New York: Viking Penguin, 1990.

Davis, Sheila. *Successful Lyric Writing (A Step-by Step Course and Workbook)*. Cincinnati, Ohio: Writer's Digest Books, 1988.

Davis, Sheila. *The Song-Writers Idea Book*. Cincinnati, Ohio: Writer's Digest Books, 1992.

Del Bianco, Lou. *Out of Rushmore's Shadow (The Luigi Del Bianco Story)*. New Jersey: Niche Content Press, 2017.

Linen, Camille Cribari. *Wolfe with an E (An Episodic Journey Through an Exceptional Life)*. Art of English, 2022.

Rolland, Romain. *Jean-Christophe*. New York: Henry Holt and Company, 1914.

Simon, Paul. *The Songs of Paul Simon*. New York: Charing Cross Music, Inc., 1972.

Sondheim, Stephen. *Finishing the Hat*. New York: Alfred A. Knopf, 2010.

Sondheim, Stephen. *Look, I Made a Hat*. New York: Alfred A. Knopf, 2011.

Voltaire. *Candide, ou l'Optimisme*. Geneva, Switzerland: Cramer, 1759.

Zollo, Paul. *Songwriters on Songwriting (Expanded Fourth Edition)*. Da Capo Press, 1991.

ABOUT THE AUTHOR

Arnold D. Cribari is a collaborative divorce lawyer and divorce mediator, and has been writing songs, off and on, since 1991. He is also a lifelong model train enthusiast.

Arnold and his wife, Shawn Kennedy Cribari, live in Yorktown, New York, and have three adult children, Maria Cribari, David Cribari and Kristina Antosik, and three granddaughters.

EPILOGUE

ODE TO THE NEW JERSEY HIRAILERS

IN THIS EPILOGUE, DEAR reader, I apply many of the songwriting process concepts discussed earlier in this book. This was done while creating a brand-new song entitled "Ode to the New Jersey HiRailers," which was largely composed and written on December 21st and 22nd of 2024 after I submitted what I thought was the completed book to my book designer, James Woosley.

On November 14th, 2024, I learned that the New Jersey HiRailers, the model train club that operates and maintains the nation's largest O-Gauge model train layout, would soon need to dismantle its massive, magnificent train layout and, hopefully, relocate and resurrect it. It took 22 years for this train club to build its current model train layout. It is an understatement to say that dismantling, moving, and rebuilding this layout is a Herculean task.

In mid-December 2024, I was discussing this task with a good friend and fellow train nut and musician, Rick Tota, fondly nicknamed Rusty Rick/Ringo Rick. He suggested that we write a train song for my wife and me to perform at Trainstock, a marvelous train show hosted by the New Jersey HiRailers at their current Patterson, New Jersey facility. We were slated to perform at this event on Saturday, January 18th, 2025. We did several train-themed songs, including "City of New Orleans" (my favorite train song written by Steve Goodman).

I hesitated because writing songs is sometimes hard work for me, and I have other priorities at this time. Also, I have already written a model train song, "Who Am I (Rollin' By)," which I performed at previous Trainstocks and will be performing at the upcoming Trainstock. I told Rick that, instead of us collaborating on a train song, I preferred that he write it and then share it with me, at which time I would give him feedback, including any lyrical ideas that might pop into my head at the moment. This would be fun to do and not work for me—and the song would be 100% Rick's.

When I had this conversation with Rick, I thought I had already completed this book. There was no Epilogue, and I had already hired James Woosley to design the book, further edit it, and get it self-published for me through Amazon.

On the evening of December 21st, 2024, I came up with a chord progression on guitar and a melody for the verse of a new song that I might, at a later time, complete.

This, in turn, reminded me of remarks by highly regarded songwriter, Jimmy Webb. He said that he usually starts writing his songs by coming up with a chord progression on piano that he finds sufficiently original and appealing, and that the melody usually follows relatively easily for him. He even said that this songwriting process (chord progression first, and then the melody) is such that he almost has to write his songs that way.

When I wrote my new chord progression on December 21st, I had a similar experience—within one hour after writing the chord progression, I wrote the melody.

When I say write, I really mean record, because I don't know musical notation. I can write down guitar chords and lyrics, but not musical notes. So to remember my melodies and rhythms, I record them using my Voice Memos app on my iPhone.

While I dreamed up this new chord progression and melody, I had no idea what the song would be about (assuming I would continue to work on it). That is unusual for me. Typically, I start a new song by coming up with a subject or title and then I either develop the music first and then the lyrics, or the lyrics first and then the music. On the rare occasion when the music and lyrics come to me simultaneously, that is exhilarating!

In the afternoon of Sunday, December 22nd, 2024 while playing my new chord progression and humming my new melody it occurred to me that January 18, 2025, is right around the corner and I better start practicing the numerous songs that my wife and I will perform at the Trainstock event. Suddenly, despite my earlier protestations, I thought that maybe I could write a song to inspire the members of the New Jersey HiRailers (I'm an associate member) to do their Herculean task. Once that happened, I couldn't help myself but write the song.

The lyrics came to me relatively quickly. I had a complete first draft of five verses, comprising an approximately three-minute story song, in about two hours. I sang the completed song to Shawn and was delighted when she smiled and told me it was good. While brainstorming with Shawn what might be a good title, she came up with "Ode to the New Jersey HiRailers." Thank you, Shawn. (By the way, about 30 years ago I wrote a funny song about our German Shephard/Beagle mix dog, entitled "Ode to Sally," so this new song is my second "Ode.")

My first impression was that, unlike most of my songs, this one would require little, if any, modifications. Usually, when I get on a roll, I can write about 75% of the lyrics and music of my songs in a relatively short time (between a few hours and a few days) and then the remaining 25% of the song might take me much more time (between two weeks and a few months) to complete. One of my songs, "Down By the Reservoir," formerly entitled the "Croton Reservoir," has been rewritten and modified by me over the course of 20 years.

Below are the final lyrics of "Ode to the New Jersey HiRailers," which appears below, followed by the QR Code so you can listen to the song while reading the lyrics. I wrote this song applying the teachings of Sheila Davis in her book: *Successful Lyric Writing*:

Ode to the New Jersey HiRailers
© 2025 Arnold D. Cribari

"We must move, will we survive? Will our train club stay alive?
Great comra-dererie, and ingenuity, Ne-w Jersey HiRailers will fore-ver be.

It will take much work and play, we can do it come what may
With hammers in our hands, and o-ur power saws,
We rip apart our dream come true, emboldened by our cause.

Once the teardown is complete, we will line up on the street,
A fleet of giant trucks, to drive on down the road.
And move our wonderland of trains to o-ur new abode.

Ode to The New Jersey HiRailers

*In our loft we artist dreamers start with easel and
canvas bare,
Paints on palette, brush in hand, the dream becomes a
masterpiece there.*

*Reconstruction will be fun, when we're done the throngs
will come,
We build the benchwork first, beers will quench our thirst,
Carefully the track we lay and cle-ar the right of way.*

*Wiring e-lec-tri-city, then play God with sce-ner-y
Great comra-derie and ingenu-ity, Ne-w Jersey HiRailers
Will fore-ver be.*

*Great comra-derie and ingenu-ity, Ne-w Jersey HiRailers
Will fore-ver be."*

You can hear "Ode to the New Jersey HiRailers" by pointing your smartphone camera at the QR Code immediately below, tapping on "Distrokid," and then tapping on the music platform of your choice (Spotify, Apple Music, iTunes, etc.).

First, regarding the subject matter and title (what John Lennon said was half the battle in writing a song), I believe the subject and title is fine considering that my purpose in writing it is to inspire the train club to do their upcoming Herculean project. However, if my purpose was to write a money-making hit, the subject and title would not pass muster because the song lacks universal appeal.

Secondly, the song's structure is relatively simple. The music of the song consists of six verses, all of which have identical music, except I added a bridge with different music to add some musical variety. The bridge is the verse in the middle of the above lyric sheet that begins with: "In our loft . . ." Beautiful simplicity in a song can be effective. An example of this is the music in "Blowing in the Wind" by Bob Dylan.

Finally, Sheila Davis says in Chapters 2 and 4 of her book that it is important to manage "viewpoint, voice, timeframe and setting" and properly use pronouns to avoid confusion and enhance clarity.

Viewpoint, voice, timeframe and setting in "Ode to the New Jersey HiRailers" is established in the first sentence of the first verse, "We must move, will we survive, will our train club stay alive?"

The viewpoint is that of the singer who tells the story of the song from the inside. He is a fellow member of the train club, and included in the "we," a first-person plural pronoun.

The voice of this story song is the singer talking to his fellow train club members.

The time frame is the here and now, in which the singer is "reacting to events that are happening now," (an expression Sheila Davis uses), and there is an urgency of time, as stated by the first few words of the lyric "we must move, will we survive…"

The setting could be various places where the singer may be in the presence of his fellow club members, but it works well for the setting to be the existing model train club facility where the members currently meet. This is the very place where my wife and I will sing the song to the audience, which will include the other club members attending the upcoming Trainstock train show.

Regarding the pronouns of the song, all of them are in the first-person plural, consisting of "we," "our," and "us." This enhances clarity and avoids confusion, as recommended in Chapter 4 of Sheila Davis' book.

Other important issues are rhyming and other poetic devices that are discussed in *Successful Lyric Writing*.

For the sake of brevity, please notice in the above-quoted lyrics that the end line rhyme scheme of the song is consistent. Note the use of alliteration. Examples of alliteration are: "we **m**ust **m**ove," "**h**ammers in our **h**ands," 'em**b**oldened **b**y our cause," and "we **b**uild the **b**enchwork first, **b**eers . . ." My affinity for alliteration may stem from my early childhood when I was enamored with **M**ickey **M**antle, **M**ighty **M**ouse and **M**ickey **M**ouse.)

The song also has some nice internal rhymes, "**ou-r power** saws," "great comrade**rie** and ingenu**ity**," "reconstruction will be **fun**, when we're **done** the throngs will **come**," "we build the benchwork **first**, beers will quench our **thirst**," and "carefully the track we **lay**, and clear the right of **way**."

In Chapter 6 of *Successful Lyric Writing*, Sheila Davis discusses rhythm. She says that rhythm or meter "is a matter of emotion," "it's instructive," "reflects the mood of its writer," and is an "unconscious choice." All of this is true in "Ode to the New Jersey HiRailers." My purpose in writing this song was to inspire the train club's army of members to succeed in relocating its huge train layout. So I instinctively and unconsciously wrote a march in 4/4 time.

The "You Got Rhythm" chapter of Sheila Davis' book will be best understood by readers, unlike me, who know musical notation. However, I did grasp, and can share, the importance of avoiding a "sing song" rhythm by varying the time value of the notes, as recommended by Sheila Davis. I believe I've done this in "Ode to the New Jersey HiRailers." For instance, in the verses other than the bridge, the time value of the notes (i.e., eighth notes, quarter notes, half notes, whole notes, etc.) is the same or similar in the first line of music, but the time value of the notes in the second line of music is different from that of the first line, and there is a variety of time values of notes within that second line. I do the same thing in the third line of music and go one step further. Specifically, in the third line of music, the time value of the notes is different from that of the second and first lines of music, and there is a variety of time values of notes within that third line of music.

My purpose in describing the above positive things about this song is not to brag, but rather to show how I applied Sheila Davis' guidance in her book to my songwriting process in creating "Ode to the New Jersey HiRailers." My intention is to help other songwriters write better songs.

Here is a flaw in my lyrics that I removed, which my stalwart feedback-giver and editor, Shawn, pointed out to me:

"Like a gorgeous girl,
Soon we will unfurl,
The ne-w largest O Gauge layout
In the World."

I removed these lyrics, even though it was one of my "darlings" (See Chapter 5). Why did I do that? First, the simile isn't a perfect comparison. A gorgeous girl does not compare perfectly with what is hoped to be the future largest O Gauge train layout in the World.

As Sheila Davis says in *Successful Lyric Writing*, if the metaphor or simile in the song isn't perfect, then dump it, even if it's one of your darlings.

The other flaw in the gorgeous girl/model train layout simile is that it could be offensive to others—particularly some women in the audience.

It turns out that I was premature when I said that the lyrics of this song hardly needed any modifications. While practicing playing the song the next day on December 23rd, 2024, I noticed that some of the lyrics were not as good as I initially thought, so I began changing them. This took about five hours during that evening—much longer than I expected. I went into an obsessive-compulsive overdrive while modifying the lyrics, which was not much fun, but now that I'm done, I'm very glad that I did it. I believe that the end product is much better than the initial version of the song. In my experience, it usually pays off to do the extra work reviewing one's songs with a critical eye to improve them.

On the morning of Christmas Eve, 2024 I played the song again and realized that some more little changes in the lyrics might improve it. I ended up spending about 4 ½ more hours making further modifications.

This was the third time I felt completely satisfied with the song, played it and then decided the song could be improved by making modifications, which I proceeded to do. Now, I have a slip file of numerous prior drafts of the song that is half an inch thick! When this happens, I wonder if the modifications will ever end. At this point, time will tell if this is true regarding this song.

CODA

Now, I feel like Colombo, saying "One more thing." I'm fascinated by the possible existence of a super consciousness of the Universe. Music, more than anything, has made me hopeful of a possible Musical and Lyrical Super–Consciousness of the Universe, and that all I need to do is tap into it, and be a conduit for it, when I write a song.

On December 27th, 2024, after sharing a homemade recording of "Ode to the New Jersey HiRailers" with Ringo Rick (my model railroader and songwriter friend mentioned earlier), and after having numerous lengthy telephone conversations with him about the songwriting process, he sent me a beautifully worded text. "The experience of songwriting can deepen the understanding of ourselves, our relationships, nature and the World." I, in turn, sent a reply text to Rick, "All very true, maybe add 'and the Universe' after the word 'World.'"

Long live Colombo! One more thing: adding the bridge to "Ode to the New Jersey HiRailers" was what turned out to be the second to the last modification I made to the song. As mentioned before, I did so to add musical variety. I started composing the bridge with a chord progression and melody that were different from those in the verses. Then, as recommended by Sheila Davis, I made the following cluster diagram to gather possible lyrical ideas for the bridge:

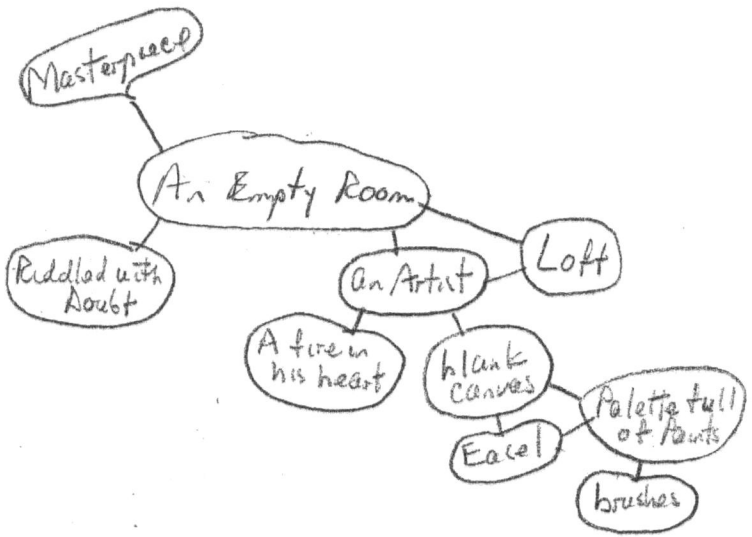

The above final lyric sheet and the recording of the song show that I included some, but not all, of my initial lyrical ideas in the above cluster diagram.

The final modifications to the song occurred when I met with my music mentor, Kinny Landrum, on January 8th, 2025, when we made a recording of the song in his basement recording studio with me singing and playing guitar, and him playing keyboard. During that recording session, I asked Kinny for his opinion about several options I had written for a line of lyrics towards the end of the song that popped into my head while driving to his home. When we discussed these options, we settled on the following line that I think is one of my best: "Wiring, elec-tri-ci-ty, then play God with sce-ne-ry." Hope you enjoy the song.

COMIN' ROUND THE MOUNTAIN (HIRAILERS)

During the weekend just prior to my January 8th, 2025 meeting with Kinny, it occurred to me that the New Jersey HiRailers' current layout has a very large mountain. That, in turn, made me think of the famous song, "She'll Be Comin' Round the Mountain," and its very catchy melody. Most of us remember the lyrics in the first verse of that song, which we learned when we were young children.

Then, the thought occurred to me that "She'll Be Comin' Round the Mountain" might be fun to do as a sing-a-long at Trainstock. I had forgotten the lyrics of the other verses of that song, so I Googled the lyrics for it and discovered that the other verses had nothing to do with trains.

What do you think I did next? You guessed it, I wrote new lyrics for the 2nd, 3rd, 4th, and 5th verses (and did so in less than two hours) to make it a train song for the New Jersey HiRailers. The lyric sheet for "Comin' Round the Mountain (HiRailers)" appears below:

Comin' Round the Mountain (HiRailers)
© 2025 Arnold D. Cribari

She'll be comin' round the mountain when she comes
She'll be comin' round the mountain when she comes
She'll be comin' round the mountain, she'll be comin' round the mountain
She'll be comin' round the mountain when she comes

When she blows her whistle she will wake us up
When she blows her whistle she will wake us up
When she blows her whistle, when she blows her whistle,
When she blows her whistle we'll wake up.

She will ring and swing her bell throughout the town
She will ring and swing her bell throughout the town
She will ring and swing her bell, she will ring and swing her bell,
She will ring and swing her bell through town.

She'll be chuggin' through a tunnel in the dark
She'll be chuggin' through a tunnel in the dark
This chuggin' train's a glory train, this chuggin' trains a glory train
This glory train is chuggin' through the dark

Us HiRailers will ride this glory train
Us HiRailers will ride this glory train
Come on board this glory train, come on board this glory train
Ride it to the Hi Railer's new home

Ode to The New Jersey HiRailers

Come on board this glory train, come on board this glory train,
Ride it to the HiRailers' new home.

Immediately after writing these lyrics, I played it for Shawn and she smiled. On January 8th, 2025, during my meeting with Kinny Landrum in his basement recording studio, he was able to immediately play it beautifully on his keyboard. Below is the QR Code so you can hear me sing it and play guitar, and Kinny play it masterfully on his keyboard.

During the evening of January 9th, 2025, I played both "Ode to the New Jersey HiRailers" and "Comin' Round the Mountain (HiRailers)" publicly for the first time at the Mohansic Open Mic, and the audience loved both songs. It's very gratifying for a songwriter like me to get such a positive response from the audience when I perform my original songs in public venues.

As I said at the beginning of this book: You can do it. If I can do it, you can do it.

Happy Songwriting!

Arnold

Published by Free Agent Press
FreeAgentPress.com
Satsuma, Alabama 36572

www.ingramcontent.com/pod-product-compliance
Lightning Source LLC
Chambersburg PA
CBHW061809070526
44586CB00024B/2774